'Nobody writes dog stories better.' Karen Charl

'This book makes you feel, respect, cherish, accep
almost makes me wish dogs could read it too,' A:

'Funny, touching, heartfelt and memorable, this i.   _ ... .iar should have
a 'must read' tag on its cover. All in all, it is a good entertaining book with a great
message.' MWB Review

'The way Jean Gill speaks for the dogs, in beautiful writing with illuminating narrative
and dialogue, I felt like I understood everything the dogs were thinking/ saying to each
other. I recognized so much of these dogs' behaviors in my own dog, which was touching.
I truly recommend this beautiful and thoroughly entertaining book!' Ulla Hakanson,
The Price of Silence

'Thank you for the wonderful experience of being in a dog's head. I've often wondered
what a dog's world was all about. Now I know.' Claire Stibbe, The 9th Hour

From the author of **The Troubadours Quartet**
Winner of the Global Ebooks Award for Best Historical Fiction

'Wonderful! If you love historical romance and adventure, you must pick up this
series!' Autumn Birt, The Rise of The Fifth Order

'Exquisitely written historical fiction.' Elizabeth Horton-Newton, View from
the Sixth Floor

'A great book! The story is so engaging, full of political issues, enemies armed with
crossbow, poison and fire, hot gossip from the ladies-in-waiting, the list is endless.'
Molly Gambiza, A Woman's Weakness

'As soon as I finished this novel, I longed for the next in the series and can't wait to
read more from this extremely talented author.' Deb McEwan, Beyond Death

'One of the best historical novels I've read in a long time.' Paul Trembling,
Dragonslayer

'A walk through time! That is what it was like to read this fine novel. It drew me into
the pages and would not let go of me until done! Bravo for a wonderful read!' Arwin
Blue, By Quill Ink and Parchment Historical Fiction blogger

Someone
to Look Up To

Jean Gill

First published 2013 (lulu)

Cover design by Jessica Bell
Cover images © Jean Gill

Jean Gill's previous publications

Novels
The Troubadours Quartet
Plaint for Provence *(The 13th Sign)* 2015
Bladesong *(The 13th Sign)* 2015
Song at Dawn*(The 13th Sign)* 2015

San Fairy Anne *(lulu)* 2010
Crystal Balls *(lulu)* 2010
On the Other Hand *(Dinas)* 2005
Snake on Saturdays *(Gomer)* 2001

Shorts
One Sixth of a Gill *(The 13th Sign)* 2014

Non-fiction
How Blue is my Valley *(lulu)* 2010
A Small Cheese in Provence *(lulu)* 2009
Faithful through Hard Times *(lulu)* 2008
4.5 Years - war memoir by David Taylor *(lulu)* 2008

Poetry
From Bed-time On *(National Poetry Foundation)* 1996
With Double Blade *(National Poetry Foundation)* 1988

Translation (from French)
The Last Love of Edith Piaf - Christie Laume *(Archipel)* 2014
A Pup in Your Life - Michel Hasbrouck 2008
Gentle Dog Training - Michel Hasbrouck *(Souvenir Press)* 2007

For Blanche-Neige de Néouvielle,
who has digested a few books in her time,
and for Bételgeuse de la Plaine d'Astrée,
who prefers household linen and
who thinks I'm God.
(Blanche still believes her day at the top will come)

Acknowledgements

With huge thanks

from Bételgeuse de la Plaine d'Astrée and Blanche-Neige de Néouvielle to Michel Hasbrouck, dog trainer extraordinaire, for all he taught their mistress.

to Blanche and Bétel's breeders for opening up to me the world of shows, the French breed club R.A.C.P. and dog breeding in all its pleasure and pain. Without their breeders, we would not have these beautiful dogs.

to all my Forum friends, especially on Patou Parle, with whom I have shared stories and problems since 2006, including Alaska, Binti, Cimba, Clo, Linda, Magali, Montagnepyrenees, Morgan, Patoulou, Sancho, Soulmans and Stratos. A special mention for the excellent breed rescue support at www.adoptiongroschiens.com My thanks to everyone who has shared a Patounien moment with me, online or at dog shows.

It is conventional to thank one's partner but not usually for still being here despite most of the bad dog behaviour narrated in the novel. As he says, 'Once you've had Pyreneans, other dogs seem to lack character.'

All the events in this novel are drawn from true stories but, apart from Michel Hasbrouck, all the characters, human and canine, are fictional. When it comes to dog problems, a lot us know very well, 'There but for the Grace of God...' I prefer, 'There but for Michel Hasbrouck...' Good dog training saves lives - dogs' lives, mostly.

IF YOU HAVE PROBLEMS WITH YOUR DOG

Read 'Gentle Dog Training' by Michel Hasbrouck and get help from a skilled dog trainer who does not shout or hit dogs.

Chapter 1

Let me show you where I was born. Shut your eyes and imagine skies so blue they dazzle, snow so white the glitter bursts against your closed eyelids, mountains dancing in the winter sunshine, dancing all the year round. In summer, the high peaks swirl their veils of heat-haze and tease with sudden nakedness to catch your breath, the chain of summits stretching beyond the horizon, whispering the ancient southern names, Pic de Viscos, Pic de Néouvielle, Pic du Midi de Bigorre, Pic de Macaupera. The shadow of a cloud drifts on the wind, lazy as a grand raptor surveying its domain, darkening an entire valley, the Val du Lavadon. I was born in the Pyrenees, with my two sisters and four brothers, seven little white rat-sausages jostling blindly to reach our mother's teats. I've seen a few pups born in this long life of mine, so what I can't remember, I can imagine. The warmth and smell of mother, the sleepy pleasure of a milk-full tummy and the newness of an outside world on this body after nine weeks growing to a curled-up ball inside my mother's baby-sac.

So much to learn... stretching, wobbling on four legs, squeaking for food, pushing Stratos off the teat I wanted (if you'd known Stratos, you'd have pushed him too), cuddling up to Snow, Sancho and Septimus to sleep in a pile of puppy fluff. The first thing I really remember was when I was about six weeks. You know how it feels when someone niggles you and niggles you; a push here, a little nip there and then one of those sideways looks just to make sure you knew it was deliberate? One sideways look too many, big brother! I can still feel that rush of power into my brains, paws and, most importantly, teeth, which sank into that plump cushion of flesh like a claw into mud. I've tried again and again to explain the pleasure of biting but words just don't do it. The first time, there's the slight hesitation as the points of your little teeth puncture the skin and then you're in! And he's squirming and squealing ... and then it all goes wrong. He's spoiling it by asking for help, real help, and he's your brother so it hurts you to hurt him and you have to stop - and you hate him for making you stop. So you've discovered how complicated life is for a dog. You can't just do what you want because the want splits in two and fights itself, confusing you.

When Stratos and I met up again, years later, and were telling our stories by the light of the moon, that was something we shared. First bite. One good thing about the animal refuge was that you did get to see the moon. If I think of anything else that was good about the refuge, I'll be sure to let you know, when the time comes. But each bit of the story has its place, time and smell, and the moment for extra-strong disinfectant, ears oozing pus and dog-breath sweet with worms, has not yet come. What Stratos and I did agree on was that the second bite was more dangerous, sweeter with the knowledge of breaking the taboo, knowing you had to be strong enough to follow through. I'm talking about biting dogs of course, not about - whisper the very words! - biting Humans. Though Stratos and I had to talk about that too, given his situation. He's my hero, you know? But as I said, everything in its own time.

So, there we were, puppy-fighting and of course Stratos bit me back as soon as I let up on him. And if you don't forget the first bite you've given, boy do you rememember the first time you got bitten, which is usually the reply to your own attempt! I was so shocked, I screamed before it hurt and then the pain flooded me with rage and I turned right back on him once more. He was shocked in his turn, and stopped biting me, with just that little shake he always gives. From then on we worked out that it was safer to stop at the squealing stage but Stratos' extra power was already starting to weigh in for him, even as a pup.

Dominant? Stratos? Maybe when he was little. When he was grown up, he didn't need to do anything. He'd just walk. And when Stratos walked you felt this urge to roll over in front of him, wag your tail, look at some far-distant imagined mountain, look anywhere but at Stratos himself. You'd want to say, 'Hey Stratos, did you skip breakfast? Here, have my throat. I don't really need it.' You'd know that once you'd cleared up the niceties of status, you'd follow him to the ends of the earth and that same big brother would protect you to the death. We were pack.

Our talents were very different and I could hold my own in some ways. Not always the brightest puppy in the pack, my brother, and he didn't get the chance to learn like some of us did. 'University of Life,' he told me later. 'Some of us learned the hard way, Sirius, and some of us ARE hard.' But even then, I wondered. What if things had gone differently for Stratos?

But that's me, Sirius, the sort of dog who wonders 'what if?' The sort of dog who started as a little rat-sausage, jostling his siblings to reach a teat, unaware that there could ever be more to life than Mother. That's something else that Stratos and I talked about - Mother, otherwise known as Morgana de Soum de Gaia. She'd been a beauty queen and even though we were dragging her down, 'draining her haggard,' she complained, there was something about the way she carried herself that said 'Princess'. She knew it and she made sure that we knew it too. 'A Soum de Gaia never does *that*,' Mother would sniff contemptuously at some puppy pee or worse fouling the straw, 'in its own den!' and then the offender would be picked up by the scruff of his neck and tossed into the yard, where the rest of us would mock and nip whoever was suffering Mother's discipline, just to show her our support. And because it was fun, of course. And doubly fun if it was Stratos in trouble and not allowed to answer us back. Not so much fun when it was your own wrinkled rolls of neck fat gripped firmly between forty-two maternal teeth and your own four waddle-paddles pedaling in mid-air, not as keen on flying as you'd thought.

'A Soum de Gaia stands like this,' she told us and made us practise standing very still, head high and stretched out a bit, front legs straight and parallel, back legs uncomfortably far back, as if you were having a stretch and then someone said, 'Hold it there!' and kept you like that. Still, practising 'the position' with Mother made it easier when Alpha Human took us one by one, put us up on a table and did 'grooming' and 'the position'. Mother had not prepared us for 'Show me your little ears,' when our Human flicked them back and rubbed them clean with olive oil.

You can imagine how much fun we had afterwards licking oily ears. I reckon we were the puppies with the cleanest ears in the whole Pyrenees. Nor were we prepared for 'Show me your little teeth'. In fact, Mother tended to be averse to seeing too much of our little teeth and had shown her own once or twice when someone really caught her teat on the raw. We didn't have much option about showing our little teeth to our Human as she put her fingers to our mouths and curled our lips back.

If you'd seen the expression on Stratos' face you'd have bust a gut laughing. I wasn't convinced he'd be a Beauty winner, even at that age; no-one checking Stratos' little teeth could look in his eyes and think how cute he was. And 'little teeth' was not the worst for the boys although at that age we weren't too fussed really. But when I look back, I do wonder now whether Humans ought to be quite so free and easy in checking out our masculinity. At the time I just thought that it was part of being a Soum de Gaia to have that tickly feeling you get when a Human puts her hands down there and checks there are two.

Perhaps I was right, because I've met a few dogs since then who feel strongly enough about their rights to consider the very idea sufficient provocation to justify the B-word. I don't know. I think you have to take their intentions into account with Humans and they mean well, you know, in their own strange way. And Stratos surprised me there. He always got that slightly glazed look in his eyes that meant he liked it. No accounting for tastes. Anyway both of us achieved the 'one, two!' tally without any trouble at all. No surprise there.

Not only was Mother a Princess, but she knew her realm from puppyhood and had grown up with most of the other dogs, the Soum de Gaia aunts, uncle and sisters. But Father was from Away and at twilight, the hour for wolf-tales before dark and real work, Mother would tell us the story of how they met and a slightly abridged version of how they mated. Amados de los Bandidos, my father. The very name was enough to make you want to run off into the mountains and howl with him, according to my mother, and she'd heard enough about him from our Human to make any bitch salivate. Amados this and Amados that and more importantly Amados for THE marriage. Even a Soum de Gaia can look at a rottweiler swaggering along the street, or the local hero with half an ear, mange and fleas, and wonder what he might be like… or so we heard during the twilight stories. But youthful fancies are only that and dynasties are founded on parents like ours, so Morgana accepted her destiny (and so should we, was the maternal message).

They met at the annual gathering, the Great Show at

Argelès-Gazost, with snow sparkling on the mountains and dogs everywhere, not just the Pyreneans, but the little Pyrenean and Catalan Shepherds, and the great Matins with their bleary, bloodshot eyes. There were music, dancing, cafés owerflowing with dogs and their owners, festive with horse-drawn tour-carts. Pennants were strung between the houses, the horses were wearing garlands, and even some of the dogs were wearing Béarnaise red and yellow kerchiefs round their necks. Apparently this was all to celebrate the meeting of my parents. And where did The Event take place? Where else but in the Show Ring of course. While she was strutting her stuff with the girls, he was leaning casually against the fence-post, starting one of those competition drools that can reach tail-length if you're lucky.

Stratos and I have discussed drool technique and he admits that he loses from impatience. At about half-tail length, the urge to shake your drool is just so strong that he can't resist it, the way the dewlaps vibrate, the ears flap, and the cool slobber sprays your scent as far as a good head-shake will send it. I have told him that if, like me, you hold out, stay very still, focus your mind on the longest stalactite of drool in history, the satisfaction of the shake is even greater but he just can't do it. Still, both of us have elicited squeals of pleasure from our masters at the quality of our drool-sprays - I've even seen mine rushing round to add some water to what I've already provided on his clothes and body. All very satisfying.

So there was Dad, starting a drool but, as I say, you need a bit of luck, and it wasn't to be. His Human had the towel clamped to Father's mouth before he'd even reached a respectable drop and, when Mother sent a flirty look in his direction, what she saw was the sheepish and sullen upper face of her fiancé, his fine head cut in two by the pink towel wiping his jaw. She says it made her laugh so much the judge awarded her 'best expression' and commented on how lively and spirited she was in the Ring. She won of course. That goes without saying. I have no intention of boring you with all the Shows and the prizes, and anyway that wasn't how my life went.

Then it was her turn to watch him and this time his Human was more of an asset. He knew she was watching and every prance, the lift of his head, every sparkle in his eye was for her and when he took his static pose, he was looking right at her with melt-your-heart-brown eyes and she was won. The judge commented on his fine aroundera and his 'star quality' as if he were performing for a special audience. You bet. For those of you new to my world, the aroundera is what we in the Pyrenees call the wheel, that high circle we make with our tails when we're happy or excited or just saying, 'Hey, world look at me'. Human words are so limited compared with what a dog can say with just its tail alone, but the gist of it is, aroundera=good mood. And the better the tail, the better the aroundera. Father's tail was perfect, a feathered curve cascading in perfect proportion but his master-stroke was to stand with his tail in repose - down, relaxed with the little hook in the end ready to rise - then when the judge looked at him, up went that tail and like the great seducer he was, my father timed the moment impeccably. He won of course. That goes without saying. I think that by this stage he was already Champion of France, Spain, the World, the Universe and Everything, so it's difficult not to be blasé about shows.

The two of them had a chance for some more personal, nose to bottom, contact while their Humans talked travel and transport, then two months later my mother headed over the mountains. Just because he had 'won her' at the show didn't mean she made it easy for him. Oh no. She enjoyed the chase as much as the next girl and the chase used every gallop of ground she could run round, every bush she could turn behind, and every insult she could hurl at him when he caught up with her. No-one would have given them beauty prizes, or dared to check their little teeth, as Mother finally stopped running away and succumbed to the oldest instinct in the world. And though she hadn't seen him or heard of him since, she left us in no doubt that his name was on our birth certificates. And what a name. What a dog. Someone for us to live up to.

'No pressure there then,' I told Stratos. Some of the others drank it all in, the shows, the father from away, the romance of a name - and nothing more than a name and your imagination - but Stratos and I, we always wanted something else. We had no idea whatsoever *what* we wanted but we were already sure we wanted something else. And we'd reached eight weeks, the age of the Choosing, when our chance for Something Else might come knocking on the door.

Chapter 2

It is a truth universally acknowledged that an eight-week old puppy in possession of an excellent pedigree must be in want of a master. There were seven of us. The girls, Snow and Stella, could be real bitches, even at eight weeks, As soon as you found a really chewy piece of straw, one of the girls would be thwacking you with a paw and whining, 'I want that' and of course if you were sleepy and couldn't be bothered to give her the snap and nose-clamp she deserved, but actually let her have the bone of contention, guess what - chewy straw abandoned within two seconds in favour of someone else's shiny pebble - as long as someone else was still interested in it. Now if I saw one of the others with something particularly interesting, I'd at least enjoy it for a while, preferably with him watching, after I'd stolen it. But that was girls for you, or at least some of them.

So it was no surprise that Snow had been jumping on straw-piles from the age of six weeks, announcing to the world that she was STAYING. She'd heard the Human discussing Which One with another Human and It Was HER. No matter how many times Mother cuffed her and told her not to think she was Top Soum de Gaia Show Queen, not for a few years yet, she sparkled her little teeth and shook her little ears for anyone who could be watching. Stratos and I worked on our drools and caught her a few times, which made us feel a bit better. And even though Mother declared that Champion Qualities have a long way to develop beyond eight weeks and - with a glare at Snow - good character is Very Important, Stella was irritated enough to compromise her own champion qualities with a sly snap at Snow's neck.

After a while, we stopped reacting. Every time Snow started, I reminded Stratos that we wanted adventures and everyone knows that adventures are elsewhere. Little did I know. And then, just when we'd grown immune to Snow chanting all the time, Stella told us She was going to Fly. Not that we were stupid enough to believe her, of course, but we rolled her in a puddle just for having the cheek to try it on. We'd seen flying. The chickens did it sometimes but not very well. Even though they were two enclosures away from us we could see them through the wire fence, squawking, clucking and flapping. Then there were the buzzards, hawks and eagles. If you were lying on your back after being rolled, you might hear a screech or a whistle and there, high, high in the sky, glided a speck. Not really what we called flying, or rather what Septimus called flying. That required frenzied activity.

My eldest brother had a real thing about flying. According to him, a jay was perfect. He liked the hop, run and power launch; he demonstrated for us, sometimes flying up as high as the apple crate. Then a hop, a run and a tease along branch, followed by a low swooping flight among the trees in the orchard, or in this case, one bounce along an apple crate, followed by a hard landing on concrete. But he still thought he could do it one day if he got the technique right and he spent hours by the fence on the left of our run, the orchard-side.

So when Stella said she was going to fly, we all thought she was making it up to spite Septimus, even though no-one could work out why. We were just sorting her out in a mass pile-up when Mother arrived. Some deft snaps, a paw to the left, a paw to the right and the puppy pile re-arranged itself into suitably cowed individuals. Of course, Stella said straight off that we were picking on her when all she'd done was tell us that she was going to fly. We waited for Mother to tell her she was too old for making up stories. All she said was, 'And?'

'And they didn't believe me,' Stella whined. At least I will say this for Snow; she wasn't a whiner. And when I met up with her later on, she tried to put in a good word... but that's jumping too far ahead.

Mother bared her teeth at us all, just a little reminder how far we could go with her - I'd estimate it at less than one claw-space. 'Stella is going to fly,' she stated. 'The Human says so.' And with that, off she stalked, ears back, tail low, clearly not in the best of moods. It would have taken a very brave or very stupid pup to chase her and play 'how far up your bum can I sink my teeth' and none of us were that stupid. Septimus slunk off to be alone and watch the orchard with his sad, dreamy eyes. When Stella was out of earshot, the rest of us discussed whether or not Stella might nose-dive when she was learning to fly, and crumple her sweet face. It wasn't as if she was likely to do what she was told... at which thought we cheered up considerably and went back to wondering what was in store for us boys.

I suppose I ought to describe our Human to you. It's difficult not to be influenced by what came later and to view events through my puppy innocence about the world but I'll try. Our Human was a female giant who towered above us, who said things and made them happen. When we started getting hungrier and Mother was snapping at us as we sank our little teeth into her tender parts, the Human brought us some very tasty new food. Of course we tried to suck on it and spluttered it all over the place. She organised us. Each of us had a bowl. If one of us tried to help himself to someone else's food, he found a Human foot blocking his way and nudging him back to his own bowl. Like Mother, she didn't like us using our little teeth on any part of her, even on the cloth she wore around her legs, and she would push us away with her feet, more and more roughly. We grew to hate her feet and we jumped away from them. We hated the broom even more, a giant stick rushing towards us and prickling our little legs. Sometimes she used the broom to push us out of the way, to 'save her shoes,' she told another Human, who often came with her to see us.

Everything was organised and she was very careful to make sure that the bowl was full of clean fresh water each day, and that we had - I think it was more than three feeding times each day - but it's a long time ago and I forget things now. I do remember that you could tell feeding time by the pointer on the farmhouse wall, and she was never late. She organised cuddling us too, picking up each one in turn, saying his name, rolling him over and tickling his tummy, smiling and laughing sometimes. Those were the good times. I've already told you about little teeth, little ears and 'the position'. At about six weeks, we met more Humans, little ones, and she told them 'good for socialisation,' and the little Humans followed the same routine of picking each one of us up, giving a cuddle. One little Human used to whisper in my ear, 'You're my favourite,' and it felt like a breath of love, a promise that something special could happen between a Human and a dog. Now, I wonder whether he said that to all the puppies.

The Human gave us some toys, fluffy dogs and plastic bones, which gave us something new to fight over. It felt good to have new textures in your mouth and it was much safer playing tug-of-war with Stratos over a blue rabbit than using your teeth on Stratos himself. The word 'blue' is interesting. You Humans don't have good hearing and your sense of smell is so bad it's useless so you've had to make up for this by developing your eyesight in strange ways. Nothing useful, like seeing in the dark, but you can see things further away than we dogs can. Even when something stays very still, and we would have to wait for the give-away movement, you can pick it out. And you Humans can discriminate colours. Unfortunately, like a city dog discovering the scents of a country walk, the average Human is obsessed with colour and goes completely off the track. So our Human thought it was important that we had different coloured toys when what we would have liked were some different scents for our noses or shapes for our mouths. We sorted it out though. We could tell the blue rabbit from the green rabbit with no problem; the blue rabbit smelled of dead mouse and the green rabbit smelled of rosemary. Obviously we all preferred the blue rabbit and the Human pointed this out to people as an indication of how intelligent we were. She was right.

With more Humans coming and going for our 'socialisation', we'd got quite used to the routine now and if someone was sleepy, it really wasn't exciting enough to wake up just for a pick-up and cuddle that we could catch up on the next time. And that's how Stratos missed his first chance. It was the very day of our eight-weeks, early afternoon and hot. And I mean hot. We were all lazing around, occasionally opening one eye to check on how far one little cloud had moved in the blue, blue sky, or sniffing a whiff of rose, cherries or cheese, whatever came our way. Stratos was flat out, lying on his back, snoring like a chainsaw. I heard the Humans coming, all those chattery noises they make, like a gathering of jays, except that jays have more sense than to group together and make all that noise. I was happily musing on why jays are better organised socially than Humans, who don't seem to realise how much noise they make collectively, when the Human's voice made a more individual impact. 'They're absolute darlings,' she was saying. 'The best litter I've ever had, so much promise, and of course they're all reserved already...' Reserved? First I'd heard of it. And she had that voice, not the one she used with the usual Humans, or with us normally. Even then, I knew it was different and now I've heard that tone again and again so I know exactly what's going on. Humans trying to win votes, Humans with their in-laws to dinner, Humans behind counters in shops.

My Human picked up Snow. 'This is the little girl I'm keeping. Look at her head...' Snow gave a sleepy crumple to show her little eyes and teeth '... and her static pose...' Hawled upright, Snow gave a version of 'the position' that suggested she would collapse back into slumber if a feather blew against her back legs. 'And this one,' the Human picked up Stella, turning her round for admiration and getting some 'oohs', 'aahs' and 'isn't she lovely' from the four new Humans, two big, two small, 'this one is spoken for.' Stella re-joined her sister, shuffled into a more comfortable position, nose tucked inside Snow's elbow, and was soon chasing sleep rabbits, back legs cycling as she raced through dream woods, where none of the rabbits were blue.

Then, to the surprise of everyone, not least the puppy she scooped up, our Human displayed Savoie-Fer to the newcomers. 'And this little boy is going to even higher mountains.' This was news to all of us. 'He's been chosen by a Breeder in the Alps as his new stud so we'll see you again at the shows, won't we, sweetie.' I'm not sure which was more shocking; 'sweetie' - which we had certainly never ever heard before - or 'stud' which we had heard often enough, usually followed by our father's name. But Savoie-Fer, or Savoie-Frère as we called him, a Stud? Don't make me piddle myself laughing.

'But as you're the first to come, you can have the pick of the other boys...' I cocked an ear but it was so hot and I didn't know the first thing about these people so I wasn't going to rush in with licks and tail-wags, was I. No, I'd just listen, think and wait. Male New Human was talking to his female and his little ones. 'Now remember all the things we talked about. It's not just which one looks the cutest, it's about character and we want a pup that's confident.'

My Human interrupted, 'Do you want me to tell you about them?'

Monsieur New Male smiled at his female, 'Thanks but we'd rather choose for ourselves,' and when he thought my Human wasn't looking, he did a funny thing with one eye, shutting it quickly and cocking his head to one side at the same time. 'Now then, you puppies.' He loomed over us, then suddenly yelled, 'Here, puppy, puppy!' in his booming voice. I was nearest to him and I couldn't help it; I jumped. The girls snuggled closer together. Sancho and Savoie-fer rolled to their feet and yapped. Only two of us were apparently unmoved. Stratos didn't move a muscle. There he lay on his back as if men shouted near him every day. He'd stopped snoring though, which told its own story. And Septimus was lying apart, totally focused on his jays, muttering his latest observations on flight to himself.

Humans have such slow reactions that I'm sure they missed what happened next. A jay took off from the orchard, jumped onto the fence by Septimus, and hopped, skipped and danced right into the middle of our pen, behind the New Humans, where it pecked repeatedly at a plank of rotting wood. The moment the jay reached the fence above him, Septimus jumped almost as high, turned in mid-air to gallop towards his flight hero. I could hear him wuffing, 'Just one little aerodynamic question,' as he used Stratos' stomach as a trampoline, knocked me to one side and Sancho into our two sisters, dashing towards his jay as if his life depended on it. Which as it turned out, it did.

'You little beauty!' declared the booming voice triumphantly as New Human scooped up Septimus before he could run past. 'See everyone? This is the Alpha Male in this litter, no question. Am I right?' and he turned to our Human.

'Yes,' she said brightly. 'I'm amazed at how you did that.'

'Experience,' he beamed, while his female said nothing. 'See the way he came when I called him? See the way he was respected by the others? See how scared the others were? This is the dog for us. We'll call him Killer.'

'Can I hold him Dad, can I, can I?'

'Cool! Killer, Killer, here boy!'

The Female's voice was quiet but cut across them with ease. 'Perhaps he already has a name, dear,' and she looked questioningly at our Human.

'Septimus. We've called him Septimus because he was the seventh and last puppy. And of course it's an S registration year.'

'So that's what's on his birth certificate,' the Female continued.

'Yes and it will be on his pedigree when you get the official form back from the S.C.C.'

'And you've been calling him Septimus so he's used to it…'

'Yes,' our Human played along happily, although as I remember, we'd been told our names but in practice were all called 'Puppy,' so at least Booming Voice had been in with a chance of us coming to our name when he shouted.

'I know Killer's a lovely name, suits him really well, but it would be a pity to waste all that early learning, don't you think, dear? And you've been telling us it's important that a dog knows its name as soon as possible … here let me try.' She took Septimus in her arms and cradled him to her, so loving you could feel the warmth just watching, and she purred, 'Timmy, who's the most beautiful, who's the best, who's the brightest, Timmy, Timmy…' and Septimus was so excited and happy - and relieved - that he piddled, narrowly missing New Female who laughed. 'Now that's a good sign.

How's about it everyone?'

Little female was reaching out already. 'Timmy,' she tried, and my brother wagged his little tail as he was passed into another pair of arms, New Female giving instructions on how to hold him.

'Yeah, Timmy's OK. Killer's good,' Little Male looked at Big Male, 'but I dunno. My friends might expect a rottweiler or something, and he's a bit white and fluffy....'

New Human shrugged. 'OK, Septimus... Timmy. But make no mistake, son. This dog will be as good a guard dog as any rottweiler - and bigger!'

'Guardian, not guard dog,' our Human corrected. 'Patous have been bred for centuries to guard the sheep in the mountains. They'll take on a wolf to protect their sheep - and their family - and that means you now.' She smiled her bright smile at the Small Humans. 'Come on in the house to do the paperwork and I'll show you photos of the spiked collars they wore in the old days to protect them against the wolves - and to keep them awake. Not a lot of people know that the collars were meant to be uncomfortable to stop lazy patous sleeping on the job.'

'There are wolves here again now, aren't there?' New Human was booming again as he and our Human headed for the door out of the compound. Quietly, the Female took Septimus in her arms and there it was again, the look and the feeling all round a Human and a Dog, that you'll never forget when you've sensed it once. You can call it Love if you like but there ought to be a special word for it. Somehow she even included the Small Humans in the whole feeling. A Family. Septimus had become a Family Dog. And I just knew he was going to be good at it. I hoped there'd be jays for him to watch. 'Good hunting, little brother,' I wuffed and the others joined in.

There was an ostentatious yawn and you could even hear

Stratos stretching. 'Have I missed anything?'

'We've lost our Alpha Male,' I told him. 'Septimus. He's got a Family now.'

'Septimus,' Stratos drawled. And lay down again, stretching his back legs out like a frog's, front legs straight out, head between them as he muttered into his paws, 'Hot today. Heat addles your brains, you know.' He couldn't even be bothered to rise to comments like 'Who'd notice the difference with you!' that someone inevitably sent his way. I often wonder, what if it had been a cold day. What if there hadn't been a jay. Would it have been me instead of Septimus? Or could it have been the real alpha male that New Human was looking for? Could he have picked Stratos? And would it have saved him? Would the Female have been strong enough?

Chapter 3

Our ninth week was a busy one. The day after Septimus left, another New Human arrived. This one didn't boom, didn't stomp and our Human used almost her normal voice when she spoke to him.

'Clever name you gave him,' she was saying as they approached us. 'I understand Savoie of course but why 'fer'?

He smiled. 'You know the old chestnut, the advice we give all our clients about training patous?'

Her brow wrinkled, then smoothed. 'Fer... meaning iron...of course! You need an iron fist in a velvet glove! Very good! You really do have the savoir-faire.' She laughed at her own joke - a poor one to judge by the reaction - then she pointed to my brother. The New Human crouched, spoke gently and held out his arms, all his movements slow and sure. I can't speak for the others but I felt as if I were being drawn towards the Human on a thread of kind words and even though I knew he was not The One, I wanted to be near him. Savoie-Fer must have felt the same, or more, because he was first to reach that outstretched hand, to sniff, accept and start licking his master-to-be. Monsieur Savoie spared some cuddles for the rest of us puppies but his eyes were only for his own. You could tell he liked what he saw. Gently, but with confidence, he checked over Savoie-Fer, who couldn't stop wagging his tail, even through the count to two, which of course he passed.

'Yes,' Monsieur Savoie said, 'Yes. He will do very well.' Our Human beamed enough to eclipse the sun and talked so fast about genes and pigmentation that I thought she'd bite her tongue when the words crashed into each other. Monsieur Savoie nodded, smiled and thought his own thoughts as he said softly, 'Come on then big boy,' and lifted Savoie-Fer into his arms. That's when I realised that Septimus had been right; a puppy could fly, in the arms of a Human. Savoie-Fer was squealing, 'Let's go! Let's go!' and wriggling dangerously, given how high up he was. But those arms were not as relaxed as they looked. Strong as iron. 'See you, Stud,' I wuffed. 'Good hunting little brother.' I didn't see him again as it happens but you'd have to be deaf, dumb and blind not to hear about him. His father's son and more. Champion of France, Spain, the Universe and Everything was commonplace in our family but Savoie-Fer added Crufts. Crossing the Channel is not as easy as you'd think; they do things differently there. And after Crufts, his puppies littered Europe. Good for you, Stud, I'd think, when I heard of yet another addition to the royal line. Next to go was Sancho. His Humans were two Females and our Human's voice reached a new pitch with them. She kept starting sentences and not finishing them. 'And the puppy is for....'

'Both of us.'

'It can only be one name on the paperwork, I'm afraid. As I always say to couples, but then that's married couples, so it's not the same is it... ah, here they are.' As if the New Females hadn't noticed five puppies the size of small bears gambolling around them

This was the first time I had seen a Human really wanting to know what the other Human thought and wanted. It was quite an eye-opener. Until then, I'd thought that inter-Human speech was mostly about saying what you wanted, or hiding what you thought while still getting someone else to do what you wanted, which came down to much the same thing by different methods. I now had to consider the possibility that Humans might be capable of generosity and unselfishness. It didn't seem likely.

We were all awake and as cute as can be that day, even Stratos, so we didn't make it easy, and there the Humans were, second-guessing each other with little testing comments. 'He has lovely eyes, don't you think?'

'But look at that patch of brown round his eyes and the freckles, on that one…'

'Blaireau,' our Human gave the technical term for badger-coloured patches on us patous. 'And red patches are 'arrouye', rusty, but I haven't got any arrouyes this time. You don't see so many nowadays, more's the pity.'

'I always thought they were all pure white?'

'No, in fact if you try to breed pure white only you'll get into problems with pink noses and, even worse, deaf dogs. There's a genetic link between deafness and lack of pigmentation. And when you know the breed, you get to like the markings as much as the pure white… I don't know why, it just seems to happen.'

'It's different, isn't it, all that … blaireau patching round the eyes, like a mask…'

'Like Zorro,' the other said, 'and I like the idea of being different.' They shared a look and our Human looked pointedly in another direction. And so Sancho became Zorro, flying off to his family in another pair of Human arms. 'May the wolves fear your door,' I woofed. 'Good hunting, little brother.'

Our Human's announcement, 'Stella's flying tomorrow,' gave us a whole day to persecute Stella and boy, did we make the most of it. She had clean tendencies, did Stella so it was pretty straightforward to wind her up; any combination of water and muck usually did the trick and Stratos and I were experts. So when the next batch of New Humans showed up, our Human was not best pleased to find her pure white girl lightly caked in dubious brown substance and if the Humans had any sense of smell at all, they'd have worked out what it was quickly enough.

A sharp intake of breath, followed by, 'I've never known her get as filthy as the last day. I swear I've cleaned her up four times and look at you again!' There was a slight hiatus in the usual look, choose, cuddle proceedings while our Human sponged down Stella, dried her and sprayed her with some revolting scent that Mother said was one of our Human's show techniques. 'There, that's more like it.' Stella shook her whole body from her ears downwards, fluffing her coat out prettily, knowing full well that the choosing had already been done (although I'd pointed out to her that people sometimes changed their minds - Uncle Diego had told me - and she'd whined with her head in her paws for ages before telling me she didn't believe me and batting me with a paw).

'And you're going straight to the airport?'

'Fraid so. We've had a few days in Paris - couldn't hop over to France without doing the Champs-Elysées,' New Human looked at his Female - 'but a few days is probably all that my credit card can cope with.' Everyone smiled.

'Don't you listen to him,' the Female put a hand on his arm. 'He's just a sweetie and I can't stop him buying me presents.' Ah. The sweetie word again. But this time it seemed at home on the lips it came from and I suppose you get used to it. Working out what it all actually means is the hard bit.

'Toulouse to Charles de Gaulles, then on home to Miami. But don't you worry about our little girl, she'll be just fine, and you know what? For the long haul from Paris to the States, you're going to go first class, up front with us, honey, where you can look through the little window and see the clouds from on top.' Stella was just lapping up every word, so absorbed she didn't notice Stratos sicking up the remains of a large beetle. In fact, you would only have known it had been a beetle, if you'd noticed Stratos chewing on it earlier. And if you'd known that one of Stratos' talents was to throw up whenever he felt like it. So with the prospect of Stella's new family coming, a bright puppy might have watched Stratos chewing on a beetle and put two and two together. Stella might not have taken any notice but Stratos made the usual noises suggesting imminent death from choking, followed by some colourful output, and certainly attracted attention from the Humans.

'No, no, don't you worry about him,' our Human's voice had gone up yet another octave. 'It's just a bit of chewed grass he's brought up.' Nobody, not even a Human, could look at what Stratos had produced and believe it to be a bit of chewed grass. Stratos was disgusted. What a waste of his artistry. They'd hardly looked at it. And he'd been hoping to provoke at least a moment's worry about Deadly Dog Diseases. But no. Our Human was rattling off again. 'Yes, checked by the vet yesterday and all perfect.' No justice in this world. Stratos was already turning away, losing interest, when the New Female reached into her pocket. 'I brought this specially for you, honey. Would I go shopping and forget our little girl?' If you had seen Stella's face as it was surrounded by a broad red ribbon, tied in the biggest bow you've ever seen! Actually, none of us, including our Human (to judge by her expression) had ever before seen a patou wrapped up like a box of chocolates. And Stella's face was a real picture, not the kind that you'd find on that same box, either!

'That should scare off the wolves, Stell,' Stratos barked at her.

'Scares the hell out of me,' I added.

As I told you, Stella was all bitch and what she answered

back put the '- Off' in 'Wo-off!'

But she was our sister all the same and whatever flying meant, it certainly included going far away, so when I saw the last glimpse of twin brown pools of hate (aimed at the red ribbon, I prefer to think), I woofed, 'Wow them Stella, good hunting little sister.' And then there were two because you couldn't count Snow. She was Staying.

You couldn't think about Choosing and adventures all the time so I gave my professional attention to Stratos' pile of sick before we both ate it. Waste not, want not.

High-sun to high-sun is a long long time to a puppy and we weren't thinking of anything other than playing swat and pounce when our Human turned up with four visitors. She was red and blotchy round her neck and her mouth was pursed tight.

'This is really not the way I like to do things but I suppose, seeing as you're all here together…'

Younger Female spoke. 'I'm sorry. We were so keen, we got here a bit earlier than we arranged… we didn't mean to put you out.'

The tight little mouth relaxed a fraction. 'Well, as long as you understand that Monsieur and Madame Larime must be allowed to choose first… it's really not at all ideal… I should have made you wait…'

'That will be fine,' younger Male contributed, looking me straight in the eyes and then switching to Stratos. 'I wouldn't be able to choose anyway - they both look superb.'

Our Human preened and bridled. 'In a good litter, there's no runt you know - and this litter isn't just good, it's exceptional. Hardly surprising of course, given the parents…'

'Oh Marc, just look at them,' said his Female, taking his arm, her eyes shining. 'They're gorgeous.' I like to remember that she said that, 'Gorgeous,' and that her eyes were shining. Some memories keep you warm even when you're frozen inside.

The Female with the glittery collar was already stroking Stratos, who'd gone into the full 'cute puppy routine', waggling his tail and back end so hard it looked as if it had come apart from the front. Then it was my turn but I still felt unsure. Perhaps I'd just wait and see. But if cuddles were on offer, I wasn't missing out so I took my share of 'What a cutie-pie' comments with good grace, despite getting a nip inside my thigh from Stratos, who promptly covered up with a neat flick of tongue.

'Oh look! His brother's washing him. How sweet! Isn't he lively!'

'Yes,' said our Human, 'Stratos is certainly lively. He'll need a firm hand, that one, an iron fist in a velvet glove'

Older Male, who was also wearing a collar, some kind of fabric, and stiff clothes that made him sweat in the sun, lifted Stratos high in the air. He looked funny and helpless pedalling his four fat little legs in the air and he cuffed me when he was back on the ground, just to make sure I didn't comment. 'Don't you worry about that.' No boomer, this one. A low, calm voice, used to being taken seriously. 'We're used to dogs, never any problems at all. The important thing is that they know who's boss and believe me, we don't have a problem with that.' He stroked Stratos gently under his chin and that was that. The minute it was clear that Stratos had been Chosen, MY Humans rushed to me and it was clear my waiting and thinking was over, so I just went with the flow and licked every single pore of Human skin I was allowed close to, while Marc encouraged me and his Female giggled because I was tickling her.

Then Stratos and I were both flying in Human arms, with Snow's goodbye wuff in our ears, and we entered The House for the Completion of Paperwork, two sets. Perhaps it's because of what came later but one bit of the very boring conversation does stay in my mind.

'I might as well say this to all of you at the same time,' our Human began, 'but only one person can be named as the legal owner of the dog, and if you split up as a couple, then it's the person whose name is on this document who owns the dog. Of course it's not going to happen to you,' she laughed and looked at both couples, and everyone laughed with her at the very idea of divorce, 'but it's better that I make it clear.' There was some light-hearted banter between the two in each couple before finally the Male Humans signed the forms. I hardly had time to wuff, 'Good hunting, little brother' before I was sitting on a fleecy blanket, on Christine's lap, with the car's engine reverberating up into my tummy, and a warm human body lulling me.

Marc was my in-writing master and I had a new family. Mother, Snow, Stratos and the others were unimaginable running and time beyond thought away from me. The mountain peaks flashed past and made me dizzy so I shut my eyes. Goodbye my mountains. What was it all going to mean? I would have to think about it later, when I woke up…

Chapter 4

'This is your new home, Sirius!' It was Marc who carried me inside and put me down gently on a tiled floor where I performed a sleepy pup's waking duty. 'Marc,' shrieked Christine, 'Take him outside quickly! Oh no! It's too late…' I ran under a chair to hide from the noise.

'See,' said Marc, with a smile in his voice, 'he knows he's done wrong. I bet it won't take long at all before he's house-trained.'

'I'll clean up - you keep an eye on him.' Once I was coaxed out from under the chair, I followed Marc everywhere. New Home was complicated, a vast nose- overload and it wasn't long before I was asleep again, curled up in the warmth of Christine's lap.

'He is cute,' she murmured over my head, in a tone I much preferred to the earlier shrieking.

'Yes,' Marc was sitting right up against Christine on the sofa, where he could reach out and stroke my ear or her hand. 'Just remember what his Breeder said though. He might be twelve kilogrammes now but in ten months' time he'll be about fifty, so don't start off habits that will make life difficult.'

'Hmmm, just for a bit though…' I snuggled up firmly while she carried on musing. 'What was all that stuff about iron fists in velvet gloves?'

'I have absolutely no idea. Perhaps we'll get a book about dogs.'

'Mmmm, or go to dog training classes. When would he be old enough for that?'

'Not till at least six months, I was told, Older, for a big dog like ours. But I'm sure we can do little things ourselves before then…'

'Like 'Give me a paw!' That would be so cute…'

Just remembering that first evening, the three of us a real family, warm as a puppy-pile on the sofa, gives me the same feeling I get with a full stomach or in deep snow. I didn't even miss the pack, my mother and the other pups, because I had a pack of my own, for keeps, and it was in writing. I had quite settled down for the night, was probably snoring, when I was rudely woken with the words, 'Time for bed, little one'. Bed?

Then I was flown through the air and landed, gently, on a big cushion, beside a cuddly rabbit, in a huge empty space swept by a draught direct from the frozen north. And, horror of horrors, even though I waddled to get back to my pack, a door was shut on me, separating me from warmth, from family, from love. You can imagine how attractive I found a cuddly rabbit, of whatever colour. I tried to be a brave boy like Mother had told me, I really did. I sang Béarnaise folk songs for a while but they reminded me of twilight singing with Mother and made me sad so the songs kept turning into laments. I sang louder and was cheered up by My Humans shouting from their sleeping quarters. At least it was clear what they wanted! So they want me to sing louder, I thought, and I did. And they shouted louder and it was much more companionable than silence alone with a cuddly rabbit. But then they stopped shouting and I got bored singing on my own.

I loved My Humans. I wanted to be with them. They were probably missing me and wondering why I wasn't with them.

This thought bothered me so much that I couldn't get comfortable anywhere. Anywhere I tried to sleep seemed so exposed, impossible to defend, and as empty as a barn with one puppy in it. Obviously, I wasn't stupid enough to sleep in a draught but I thought the cushion might be useful all the same. I needed something to chew and that would do for starters. Once I'd sucked a corner really really moist, I sank my teeth in and did double-time chewing, the sort that had really ended a fine relationship with our mother's teats. Within seconds, I'd got into the real meat of the cushion, soft yellow honeycombed stuff that was bouncy against your teeth and just melted in your mouth if you chewed and swallowed a bit. The greatest pleasure was in just ripping the stuffing to shreds and it was so soft, I could use my claws as well as my teeth. I'd soon decorated my sleeping-room with shreds of yellow foam. And then I was bored and lonely.

I loved My Humans. I wanted to be with them. They were probably missing me and wondering why I wasn't with them. A Soum de Gaia is resourceful. I would tell them that I was shut away from them and needed help to join them. I had communicated with them already by singing but they hadn't quite got the message. I needed to try something else. The only thing that stood between me and the warmth of Christine's lap was the door. So I would try to get through the door and make lots of noise so they would know I needed help to succeed. If I managed to get through the door on my own, so much the better and they would be so proud of me. Teeth were no use on the door as they couldn't get a purchase on the smooth surface and I couldn't reach the handle. So claws it was.

I stood on my hind legs and scrabbled like mad at the door, scraping my claws down it to see if I could get it to open. I whined to tell My Humans I needed help. After what seemed to be a very long time, they shouted some encouragement to me and I doubled my efforts on both the whining and the scrabbling. Eventually, just when I was about to give up, my little paws aching from such hard work, I heard Human movement and I only just stepped back before the door opened. It had worked! Marc was there! He wasn't very pleased. Perhaps he'd expected me to open the door without his help but I was only eight weeks old. I would just try harder another time and see if I could please him.

'Oh God, no,' Marc said, surveying my sleeping room. 'I'll sort it in the morning.' He was clearly realising that this was not the right place for me to spend the night. He had understood me. And even better, he flew me through the air again right onto the carpet beside the bed he shared with Christine. 'Just for tonight,' he said.

'Well I can't take any more tonight, that's for sure, and as for what the neighbours think!'

'Night, night, Izzie. Go to sleep, for God's sake!' Marc's hand dropped down beside the bed onto my head and caressed me. I curled up on a slipper close to the deep dark of under-bed and chewed myself to sleep.

And so began my attempt to understand and communicate with My Humans. I had some successes. I'd been told I was too big to get on the couch. They were mistaken and I showed them that in fact I could get onto the couch more and more easily. They pushed me off. I got back on. They pushed me off and said 'No.' I got back on. And so I taught them how to play 'push and jump'. They pushed me off the couch and I jumped back on. This was pretty good as games go and made me realise that Humans could be taught. You just needed a bit of determination. And if they got it right even once, then you knew that perseverance would get you there.

An example of this was when I taught them to open the door for me. After my success with one door, I tried others.

I'd be outside in the garden when they were in the house and I'd want to come in, perhaps because I needed a pee for instance. So I'd scratch at the door and whine. At first Marc didn't get it. He said, 'I don't want him scratching and whining to come in so just leave him there.' I just persevered, knowing one of them would get it eventually. It was Christine who let me in the first time. And from then on, I knew that if I kept it up, someone would let me in. Sometimes, I had to keep trying for ages. Marc said, 'This is getting worse. We've got to stop letting him in when he does that.' And I had to really treble my efforts to get through to them. I was even left outside a few times until they decided I could come in! No way was I having that and I just put in the extra work needed until Christine was smart enough to let me in, and then it just got easier and easier. 'If we're going to let him in anyway, we might as well do it before he destroys the whole door,' she told Marc.

Training them to walk properly was a lot easier. After the early weeks of full pack hunts, Christine gave up on walking with us because she had 'Things to Do'. Marc and I adjusted to being the whole pack but he had so much to learn. I accepted the collar and harness he put on me but in return I expected some understanding and so I was hard on him. If he didn't stop straight away when I wanted him to, I jerked him sideways. If he walked too fast or jerked me, I sat down and wouldn't budge until he gave me a treat (I was very partial to the brown ones that smelled of rotting fish). I tried to socialise him by yanking him across to say hello to every human or dog we passed. And I encouraged him to stick up for himself more. If a dog hurled insults at us, I returned them, hoping that Marc would join in but he just wasn't that sort of male, so I did it for him. Then, when I'd had enough walking, I'd just turn right round and Marc quickly learned that it was time to go home. One time, he wanted to walk further than I did but I really wasn't having this sort of insubordination so I just lay down and let him jerk away on the harness, which wouldn't have had any effect on a flea, until he got the message. Lead work became much easier as I grew bigger but by then Marc was pretty well trained anyway.

Another great success was food. I was not just a growing dog but a growing patou, putting on between one and two kilogrammes a week, according to the box Marc stood on, holding me. I was permanently hungry. I suffered an initial setback in food training when Christine decided to stick with the amount of food suggested on the packet of dried food and no amount of salivation over an empty bowl convinced her to give me seconds. 'It doesn't even look like real food,' she said, 'but the vet says it's good for you.' However, there is always another way for a determined puppy. My masterstroke was the pleading look when Christine and Marc ate. I didn't say a word, I didn't bat a paw, I just looked at what they were eating and reminded them of what I had been given to eat. 'I feel guilty,' Christine said. 'It wouldn't hurt to give just a little scrap...'

'No,' said Marc. 'We said we wouldn't' But I kept at it, and I didn't have to act because when I sniffed cooked chicken, freshly baked bread, cheese sauce... the taste buds were feeding the brain all right and the lust in my melting brown eyes was genuine enough. 'Just this once,' by now my favourite words, and from then on I passed from Christine to Marc under the table, nuzzling for the goodies that didn't always come but often enough for me to keep working for them. And sometimes I was lucky enough to have extra Humans at the table. Little Humans were the best to scrounge off - even if they didn't give me something at the table, they would smear food on their clothes for me to tuck into afterwards. 'He's wonderful with children,' Christine said. 'He'll lick them all day if they let him.'

And bark-training was just a doddle. I applied what I'd learned that first night when we'd sung together. Someone went past the gate; I barked. If I kept on barking, Christine or Marc, or better still both of them, would shout and there we were, all three of us barking. If a dog went past the gate, I'd bark loudly and fiercely, they'd shout louder and there we were, all three of us suitably defensive of the pack and I'd hardly had to work on it at all. Teaching them to respond to the play-bark was equally easy. I'd bark and drop the squeaky ball at their feet. No go. I'd bark for longer and drop the squeaky ball at their feet. 'I don't want him barking because he wants to play,' Marc told Christine, so I had to be patient. I barked and barked and dropped the squeaky ball until, 'Oh all right then' was followed by the ball being picked up and from then on, they'd got the message. Sometimes I had to bark longer than others but they always understood in the end.

But I had some failures. There was a convenient spot in the corner of the room I had first slept in, the kitchen, so I continued to use it as exactly that - a convenience. It smelt just right and made it easy for me to squat and piddle. But as soon as Christine or Marc saw me start to squat they grabbed me and rushed me outdoors. Why they thought I wanted to go out of the house at such a moment I don't know. Of course I would have to hold it all in patiently until they took me back inside do I could dash to my corner and oooooooh, the relief! But then they'd start up again with taking me outside. The only good thing about all of this is that sometimes I *did* fancy going outside to play in the garden, have a sniff around, so of course all I had to do was squat, or pee, and hey presto! they'd take me out.

They did try hard. Christine even made my corner smell even more inviting, like someone else had been piddling there too. I heard her telling Marc, 'I've put enough bleach down to disinfect a pigsty but it's not working.' I wish I could have put her mind at ease and told her that it was working really well, if only they'd stop taking me outside all the time.

Another major failure was in getting them to take me everywhere. I loved my Masters. I wanted to be with them. And they kept leaving me. Believe me, I worked on it. Every time Marc went to the bathroom and shut the door on me, I scrabbled at the door and whined until he came out. I could tell he felt the same anxiety at our separation because when I jumped all over him, he showed the same joy at seeing me again, cuddling me and telling me everything was all right. Sometimes one or both my Humans went completely out of my awareness, shutting me in the house when they left it. 'There, there, Izzie,' they said. 'You'll be all right.' No-one tells you that you'll be all right unless there's something bad to reassure you about so I started panicking before they left. Without me to look after them, anything could happen. And you could tell they were scared because as well as all those reassuring words, they lingered, cuddling me, afraid they'd never see me again. By the time they actually went out, I was in such a state that I had to chew something to calm myself down and just when a chair-leg or a chunk of skirting board had restored my Zen, I started thinking about them coming home, how they'd jump around with excitement when they saw me and that made me want a pee and then I needed to chew again.

But it was all worth it when they came home. We exploded with the pleasure of seeing each other and I customised Christine's back or Marc's shirt-front with pawprints. 'He's just so excited to see us,' Marc said, 'you can't tell him off.' And I ran twice round the garden with excitement, crossing a new mudhole before returning to thump my masters in the chest with my front paws. I never did get them to take me with them but at least the homecomings became more and more spectacular, to the point that I could knock one of them over while the other ran into the house and gave me the fun of the chase.

Ah, the innocence of youth. I look back on my puppyhood with so many mixed emotions. So many pleasures for teeth and tongue to discover; the firmness of oak (a table leg), the pleasing give of pine (the bottom stair), the sharp prickle of splinters against your gums when you manage to suck a wooden corner right off; the chalky dust of plaster when you've scraped a long hollow down a wall after the pleasing crackle as you strip a little torn wallpaper with your teeth; the way fabric goes gooey when you suck it, especially wool. And if the fabric had that spring-flower-and-female-sweat smell of Christine, sheer bliss. If the weather was fine, Christine would hang some clothes up on a line for me to help myself to something I fancied. I remember spending a happy morning with a very chewy dress that she said was one of her favourites. It was wonderful that she could share this with me and I made it last as long as I could, but that's difficult for a full-blooded male. The instinct to gulp your pleasure turns your brain to a wasp mid-sting, unstoppable.

I became discriminating. I discovered underwear, preferably worn underwear, but even washed underwear still carried the scents dogs dream of. I taught Marc and Christine to play chase. Just to see their little faces as I flirted a pair of knickers just out of reach round the bushes in the garden was worth the effort of timing my break-in (I wasn't 'allowed' in the bedroom during the day), and sneaking my contraband outside. And I've always believed that it is a dog's duty to give his masters exercise; what could be better than running around outside, chasing your underwear? Humans generally don't run round enough.

Another advantage of this game was that it could easily be extended to visitors. Christine enjoyed making the game more difficult to add to the pleasure. 'Watch out for the dog,' she told New Humans. 'If he can get your underwear, he will.' Never one to duck a challenge, I'd listen for the way they shut the guest room door. Click meant no go. No click and that meant All systems go! The door might look shut but all you had to do was apply some Pyrenean muscle in exactly the right spot and hey presto, lingerie-on-the-field day. Obviously a break-in was puppy-play if no-one was in the house but me, especially as I could by now open the door of any room they shut me in by using my front paws to push the handle down, but where was the fun in an underwear chase on your own? No, the sport was in the show, 'Here Humans, look what I've got,' and the chase. I hardly even chewed my trophies and mostly they re-appeared on the washing line to play another day.

My serious chewing, I saved for my one big weakness. I needed a high fibre intake. I needed roughage. I was ranging the kitchen, licking worktops and investigating smells when I noticed an appetizing odour blending bread, cooked beef and stale milk with soap-and-vinegar. There were actually dozens of scents stewed over time to an irresistible temptation that I tracked to a square sponge that Christine had left for me right by the sink. I didn't have to be asked twice but as it was too good to chew, it went down in one. That was the start of a puppyhood addiction that lasted a year.

'Oh no,' Christine shrieked. She was a very loud, high-pitched Human. 'He's had the washing-up sponge again.'

'You'll have to put it higher up.' That was Marc, raising the game once more, to make sure I kept learning and improving. Of course after that, I had to stand on my back legs and look higher up for my fibre supplement. 'It's dangerous for him to eat things like that. It could block his stomach, cause an occlusion.' He needn't have worried. What went in, came out, looking much the same actually. This became such a routine that Marc would clean up the garden, then go into the house and say, 'Pink,' or 'Green' and Christie would acknowledge the re-appearance of yesterday's missing washing-up sponge.

And then I took fibre a stage too far. I'd enjoyed chewing the oven gloves, with their char-grilled taste and the intense pleasure of foam interior but they'd been hidden somewhere I hadn't found them yet so I discovered something else.

'Have you seen the tea-towel, Marc?'

'Oh, no.'

I couldn't settle that night. I felt like I needed to go to the toilet so I whined and was told to shut up. 'You've cried Wolf once too often you have.' This was a bit unfair as it was my job to cry wolf and I'm willing to bet there were no wolves within ten runnings of our house - all down to me. But just when it mattered, they weren't taking me seriously. And this was serious. My guts were bubbling like a volcano after thousands of dormant years. I knew I was going to blow. And sure enough, my stomach erupted and I found out what it was like to really heave up. Not the little grass sickies that Stratos and I had self-induced but a full blown 'If I don't bring up this tea-towel, I'll die.' I'd made it out of the bedroom into the hall and Marc was there beside me, all concern now. After a few indeterminate piles on the floor, there it was.

'The tea-towel,' Marc yelled to Christine.

'Oh good,' was the sleepy reply.

One end might have finished evacuating but the other was about to start and when I ran to the outside door and whacked it with my paws, Marc took me seriously, thank Dog. I finished my business and went back to the bedroom, carefully wiped my bottom on the carpet and flaked out, desperate for some sleep. I half-heard Marc coming back to bed after clearing up.

'He smells foul,' Christine murmured.

'I'll clean him up in the morning.' Then silence.
The tea-towels went to live with the oven gloves.

Chapter 5

'I thought you were going to make him sleep somewhere else after a bit.'

'But he's happy here. And you know what he'll be like if we try and move him now...'

'He snores, he farts, he walks about in the middle of the night and shakes his ears. He's noisy when we make love. He puts me off. It's like having a dirty old tramp watching us.'

'You're imagining it. He's not interested at all in me doing ... this... and this... See, he hasn't moved a muscle...' Marc initiated that strange courtship ritual Humans perform. Amazing smells though. I vibrated my dewlaps to maximise the scent discrimination. How do you Humans live with the handicap of your nose?

'He's waggling his face.'

'You're imagining it. Shut your eyes...' My eyes were already shut. I was all nose.

'Marc...'

His warm, purring, afterwards voice. 'I love you too...'

'No, it's not that... you said you were going to take him to classes and he's eight months now.'

'I think he's pretty good...young of course but pretty good.'

'But you said...'

'Mmmmm, OK, no problem... we'll go to classes... show them how it's done...'

So we started dog classes. Christine didn't go because she had 'Things to Do.' Marc and I were in total agreement over one thing; we didn't need training. I had no doubt that I had established myself firmly but kindly as leader. I had no need to nip him or growl at him, or any other Human, and it was my strong belief that only stupid or scared dogs needed to bite Humans to keep them in order. I was so secure in my leadership that I indulged Marc by rolling over and letting him stroke my tummy. 'Look,' he told Christine, 'that's a subordinate position because he's making his throat vulnerable.' Marc had indeed been reading dog books.

Sometimes Marc behaved inappropriately. He would use a cross voice or even shout and wave his arms about. 'Ignore him,' he told Christine. 'That's the best punishment.' So I would ignore him until such time as I decided would be the right moment for a good leader to forgive his subordinate and allow him to become pack once more. I would go to Marc, whack a paw across his forearm, if he was sitting down, or across his thighs, if he was standing, and I would look deep into his eyes, explaining to him that this was not how he should behave and I hoped he'd learned his lesson. 'See,' Marc told Christine, 'he's come to says he's sorry. He knows that what he did was wrong.' And then he'd give me the cuddle I'd demanded from him and all would be well between us again.

We'd worked on the 'command' words. It all seemed fairly straight forward to me. If I was in the mood for a treat, I could respond to Marc's special words, 'Sit', 'Down' and 'Come here' by carrying out certain actions. Once I'd got the treat, I did what I liked. If I didn't feel like a treat, I did what I liked. It was all good fun. I'd learned to be wary of 'Come here' as Marc would abuse it if given the opportunity. Just when I thought I'd taught him that 'Come here' meant he should give me a treat and cuddle me, or even throw the ball for me to play with, he used 'Come here' to trick me into the house to be shut in while they went out. I wanted to stay in the garden and I was not pleased. So next time I heard 'Come here' I checked carefully whether he or Christine had going-out shoes on before I went anywhere near him. And if he wanted me to go in the house, he could chase me round the garden and catch me first.

He was understanding 'Come here' very well at the stage he started taking me to the park. There, he explained to me that I'd been such a good dog I was allowed off the lead, but if there was any monkey business I'd be straight back on it. Off lead was fun. Like being in the garden but further to run away. When I heard 'Come here!,' I felt like a treat so I ran to Marc, enjoyed a doggy chocolate drop and - hey, what's this? Quicker than you can say, 'end of fun', the lead went back on. 'He was brilliant on the recall,' Marc told Christine.

Next time we went to the park, I was off lead and I mean OFF. 'Come here!' rang in my brain and I looked at Marc. Treat? Nice but. Could he be trusted? Sadly, no was the answer. I felt like playing off lead much longer so I ignored him. He was right about that. Ignoring was a very useful punishment, and kind. I taught Marc to call me several times until I felt like returning and claiming my treat, or, even better, to chase me round the park the way he chased me round the garden at home - and catch me when I felt I'd had enough. Yet again, I was fulfilling my responsibility to give him exercise and I was proud of myself.

So we didn't need training classes but I felt our mutual understanding was good enough for us to have some fun there. My confidence was dented just a little when faced with five Belgian Shepherds, three German Shepherds, one rottweiler and two cocker spaniels. I thought I'd talk to the spaniels while we were all waiting for puppy class to end and adult class to begin.

After exchanging anal and nasal pleasantries, we got onto the nitty gritty. 'We're old paws, came up through puppy class,' explained the black cocker.

'Starred in the exhibition,' chimed in his golden friend.

'Part of the annual village fête for the Saint's day. We practised for weeks and we were the best in class for noses. Could find THE hankie in a laundry.'

'THE stick in a forest.'

'THE biscuit in a bakery'

'Show us the object, give us a sniff and we follow our noses.'

'Noses never fail.'

'So on this particular occasion, it was business as usual, just like in class. There was a pile of national flags and all Neu had to do was pick out the French flag, tricolour they call it, pre-sniffed of course. He was chosen because he's black.'

'Not because I'm better, no, no, no, we work together when we can - Casper leads and I follow, checking for false trails. What we'd really like is to work for the drugs squad, preferably at an airport, but I don't think our Human is up to it and so we have to do our best with the Handler we have.'

'Anyway, there was Neu, in the middle of the field, surrounded by all the villagers and tourists. My master was right at the edge of the field, as if he was giving instructions but we all knew that Neu had it in the bag, without needing any encouragement. Neu had the tricolour in his teeth, gently so as not to tear it, the crowd 'oohing' and 'aahing' a bit so Neu teased them a bit longer, then that scent hit his nostrils. You could see his face twitch.'

Neu's face obligingly repeated the motion 'Sausage,' he reminisced, 'in a burger bun. And I wanted to show them a bit more for their money. Anyone can do the tricolour.'

'But only my brother could have retrieved a hot dog from the beer tent and come back for the flag! From the moment he ran off the field and into the tent I could see his plan and I was barking myself hoarse telling him to go for it!'

'But it was not to be. I told you our Human just isn't bright enough. He caught me when I was on my way back for the flag, with the hot dog in my mouth and he growled me out for leaving the field. The crowd was laughing and cheering, Casper here was cheering me on, but the moment was lost. My master held onto me and I couldn't get back to the flag for my grand finale. It's hard to forgive them sometimes but you have to remember how limited their faculties are. What about your Human?'

While we were swopping stories about our Humans, I kept half an ear on the conversation between the sources of our many disappointments. A good patou always has half an ear for what his master's doing.

After they had performed the hand-shaking and verbal pleasantries, they got down to the nitty gritty. 'Yes, I'm an old hand,' the cockers' master, François, told Marc. 'My two are very talented, especially for tracking, but easily distracted. I want to keep going with basic obedience as well as some of the further training, so we're back here again. You're after the basic?'

'Yes, the basic will be just fine for us.'

'Well if I can channel some of the enthusiasm these two put into the wrong things, I'll be a happy man. I could have killed them last week but I'm starting to see the funny side now. We live out in the wilds, no-one within miles,'

'That would be useful.'

'A barker huh?' Marc nodded. 'Well the disadvantage is that we're a sitting duck for burglars and last week it happened. We came home and found a window smashed and all the electrical stuff gone, and the house completely trashed, stuffing coming out of furniture, books torn and thrown around, just sheer destruction. At the time we were relieved when we found the dogs were still there, safe and sound, and asleep in their beds.

Then the police came, did their little bit of forensic, and we found out why the dogs were so tired. It was the dogs that trashed the place. As far as the police can work out, the burglars smashed a window, entered, took the white goods and left through the door. If they had any contact with the dogs at all, then it was probably some attempt at friendly play. For whatever strange dog logic, the burglary triggered off some desire to join in or something, or stress at strangers being there, who knows… anyway, trash the place they did. I don't know if the wife is ever going to forgive them for that… one reason we're here is to get them out of her sight for an hour. '

'Oh, my Christine just adores Sirius. We've had him from a puppy you know. He's still a puppy now really.'

'A puppy. Right.'

'He might be a bit bigger than your average but he's still going to be a puppy in his head until he's at least two.'

'Perhaps you should take him to puppy class then! But I'd pity the other pups! Speaking of which, that's the puppies going. We're on. Come on, boys. Good luck, Marc.'

The trainer, a woman of medium height, held a bicycle horn, which, we were told, was the signal to the masters to give whatever command word she instructed. So it was supposed to go something like this; trainer pumps horn - beep beep noise and trainer says, 'Tell your dogs to sit' - master says, 'Sit' - dog (me) sits - treat and praise - dog (me) gets up.

'No, no, no, Marc - your dog mustn't get up until you tell him to. You need to have a release command.'

'I do? But I've never had a problem with him getting up or carrying on after a command.'

'I haven't got time to explain now Marc, just do it please.'

Ten pairs of canine eyes all turned in my direction. The honour of a patou was at stake. We walked around the ring again until 'Beep-beep-beep' and I didn't wait for the rest, I sat - I'd show these B. Shepherds how sharp I could be if I wanted to and I would be straight up again after my treat. Unfortunately, Marc also felt challenged on the honour stakes, so when I tried to get straight up, he kept saying, 'Stay, stay, stay,' and pushing down on my rear end like it was a burger in a bap. Well, I just pushed right back and then skipped sideways so the two us sprawled in a heap with him saying, 'He didn't get up, though, did he.'

The trainer was shaking her head and we now had the attention of everyone in the room. 'He mustn't sit down when the beep goes, Mark, but when YOU say the word, and then you only give the command ONCE. And you need a command word for the release. Try 'enough' or 'thank you'.

'How's about 'nightmare'!' muttered Marc, then more loudly. 'So let me get this right. If he sits down too soon, I have to stop him sitting down, then I have to make him sit down at the right moment, then I have to stop him getting up, then I have to make him get up at the right moment and the right moment is whenever I say the right command word? Right?'

'Exactly. Now I know you're new Marc, but everyone needs their share of attention so perhaps you can just try your best?' Marc tried his best. To be honest, I was getting a bit confused what with beeps and the trainer using our special words, then Marc using our special words and then all those sits and ups were losing me a little until the moment Marc yelled, 'Sit Down, God damn it!' and then I was completely lost. Every eye in the room was on me and I didn't have a clue whether he meant 'Sit' or 'Down' so I waited a minute for clarification and then took a guess and lay down. 50:50 chance and I guessed wrong, or so I figured as Marc tried to haul me back

into a sitting position. He'd told me at the vet's that my
current weight was 45kg and he'd seemed quite proud of that
at the time but he was sweating now.

'Time for a switch. Let's try recall,' said the trainer. 'OK, in
pairs, please. Marc, if you watch the first pair, you'll get the
idea.'

We all stood at one side of the hall then one by one, each
master gave his dog to someone else, went across to the other
side of the room, called the 'Come here' or something a bit
like it and the dog was let loose to go to its master and get a
treat. Boy, those Shepherds were keen and even the spaniels
were hot under the paws to cross that room. Then it was our
turn. Monsieur Cocker took my lead and Marc walked over
to the other side of the room.

'Here boy,' he called. 'Come here, Izzie.' His voice shook a
bit. 'There's a good boy,' he pleaded.

The lead dropped, I started towards Marc, just from habit,
not rushing of course. I wasn't a Shepherd and I needed to
think this one out. I had already taught Marc 'Come here' - it
meant I went to him if I felt like it and I got a treat. What was
in it for me to cross that room to him? I couldn't find a good
answer to that. Why had the other dogs done it? That was an
easy question. Either they didn't have their masters properly
under control so they felt they had to genuinely do what they
were told, *every time* (perish the thought) or, Theory 2, they
were getting better treats than I was. No, the more I thought
about it, the better it would be for Marc's training if I didn't
go to him. I needed to make it clear in front of all these
Shepherds who was boss in our house, so I walked half-way,
just to make it clear that the command was understood all
right, so we could use it again another time if I wanted to, and
then I headed off to say hello to a pretty Belgian at the far
end of the row. Marc kept up his 'Here Sirius' for a bit until
it became obvious that I wasn't going to go anywhere near

him and then the trainer moved over to join him.

'Once only for the command, Marc, and say it as if you mean it. Let me show you. What's his name again?'

'Sirius.'

'Right. Sirius, come here.' She snapped it out nicely, even if she did use my long, I'm cross-with-you name, and her own Belgian Shepherd sat bolt upright in the corner where he'd been minding his own business since he'd been told to stay there. When he realised that he wasn't the one being called, he lay down again peacefully. I remembered Theory 2 so I ambled over to the trainer to check it out. 'Good boy!' She gave me the same old treats I'd been getting from Marc and I still remember the disappointment. That was the last time I'd come when *anyone* called me, unless I felt like it.

'We'll call that the end for today,' announced the trainer, beaming. 'You know what you need to work on for next time, Marc, and I'm sorry but we just can't afford individual attention, you know. Some of the others here are moving on to agility and I wouldn't be surprised to see some of these names figuring right up there among the best.'

'Thanks,' said Marc.

That night, we gave up waiting for Christine to come home and she woke us up when she did.

'You're late.'

'You know what the girls are like. How did class go?' asked Christine, as she climbed into bed.

'Great,' said Marc, 'but you were probably right not to come. I think you'd find it boring.'

'I'm sure you're right, darling. And I have so much to do, anyway…. no, don't do that… I'm really tired…'

Chapter 6

'He's taken over our life, Marc. He chews everything, he steals everything and he still pees round the house! At nine months!'

'He's not peeing. He's territory-marking now he's an adolescent. He's got all the testosterone kicking in.'

'You can do as much male bonding as you like but it looks like pee to me, it smells like pee and it sure as hell has to be cleaned up like pee!'

'Give Christine a paw,' Marc told me, so I did. And I cocked my head on one side to give her a sideways look. That usually did the trick. But today I might as well have cocked my leg, and over her, to judge by the reaction.

'Go away, Sirius'. The words were accompanied by a shove. Ah, she wanted to play. I shoved her back. 'See,' she shouted, 'he won't do anything he's told. Nothing!' And she left the game and the room, while I wagged my tail, hoping to calm the atmosphere. I looked at Marc.

'Come on boy. Let's go out,' Now that really got the tail wagging and we walked and walked, sharing our thoughts on Christine for a long time. Hormones, we agreed. Hers, not mine.

When we got back to the house, the kitchen table was set for lunch and Christine seemed much calmer. The phone rang and Christine rushed to answer it while Marc went to hang his coat up. Naturally, I investigated lunch. I could hear Marc heading back to the kitchen, so, a bit short of time, I selected some cheese.

'Oh, no you don't,' Marc moved the cheeses out of reach and sat down to guard the table. I couldn't say a word. My mouth was full of the most wonderful milky, fruity, salt taste I had ever known but unfortunately my teeth had sunk into the cheese and stuck solid. I couldn't move my tongue. How was I going to breathe? No sooner had the thought occurred than I needed to and I couldn't. 'Wmppp,' I tried to tell Marc but no sound arrived. 'Wrrrrt,' I tried again. He didn't even look at me.

'See you Tuesday then.' The telephone clicked back into its holder and Christine was actually humming to herself when she came into the kitchen.

'Who was that?'

'Marie.' Christine sat down to eat, oblivious to my silent pleas, even though I stood there, quivering. She looked at the cheeses. 'Where's the Beaufort?'

'Ah,' said Marc. I was out of the room for a minute and I think Sirius might have had a little bit of cheese...'

'Marc!' Christine was shrieking again. She did that even more these days. 'It wasn't a little bit! It was a slab of Beaufort.' She turned to me, her eyes narrowing. At last. I wagged my tail, desperately, hopefully. 'Oh my God, it's still there! Look at him - he's got cheeks like a hamster's.'

'You big idiot,' Marc told me, as he prized open my jaw and stretched it enough to remove my trophy. I tried for a snatch at just a little bit as it flew out of reach but I was too late. It broke my heart to see all that wonderful cheese going out of reach, into the bin. I'd have to work on jaw-strengthening exercises before going for anything that big again but it would be worth it. I licked all the bits stuck in my teeth and was licking them again when I heard a sound I hadn't heard for a while. Christine was laughing. Better still, Marc joined in and the two of them leaned against each other for support, pointing at me and laughing some more. Humans. No understanding them. I just carried on licking my teeth.

Marc and I kept going to training classes. The best bit was catching up on gossip while we waited for the puppies to finish. Some of the Shepherds had interesting stories to tell even though they seemed a bit driven in everything they did. Everything was a competition; who could sit the fastest, who could catch a ball without it bouncing, who could hear a mouse squeak a thousand miles away. They probably competed in their dreams. But I was way ahead of them in training Humans and I was so proud of Marc, I felt I could indulge him by responding to the command words most of the time. He was happy and the trainer kept holding Marc up as a shining example of how well her methods worked. Life couldn't have been better.

Each time we went out for a walk, the ground smelled more of mouldering leaves and if there was a strong wind, trees would shake the leaves in a storm around us as we walked, a crunch or a squelch underfoot as we walked, depending on the weather. It was warm but no longer too hot and the rivers had filled up again so they were 'healthier' according to Marc. We met up with new friends, a Newfoundland and his Human, someone from Marc's work.

The first time we met up, we walked the path by the river, where sweeps of pebble border merged the ripples with the land. It had been some time since I'd met a dog the same size as me, never mind bigger, and the relief of playing no-holds-barred was so great, I was in the water before you could say, 'Wet stuff.'

'Marc,' I howled, 'drowning!' but the two Humans were continuing along the path oblivious to my head going under for the third time. And then the scruff of my neck was pulled, shaken and I came up for breath once more. My legs were automatically paddling like a chicken's in a fox's mouth and I found that if I kept my head low in the water, just nostrils out for breathing, instead of struggling to get my head as high as possible, I could at least keep breathing.

'Like this, dummy,' Porthos told me, as he struck out for the middle of the river. If you've never seen a Newfie swim, you should. And what a teacher! It's not just webbed paws they have, it's water on the brain. They're in their element and they know it. 'Hey, watch me Sirius!' and he lunged with all the power in those shoulders, stretching his muzzle to grip a dead branch with his teeth and shift it from a rock cleft into mid-flow. He shifted his teeth to one end of the branch, directing the other end nearer and nearer my mouth and I took the hint. There we were, clamped onto a branch, going with the flow. Dog, but it was fun. 'More power to your back legs and less splash,' he'd yell. 'Splash is just for fun. Don't do an aroundera in the water for Dog's sake!' Porthos just kept inventing games and improving my technique and it's quite possible that we really didn't hear our masters the first four times they yelled 'Come here!'

'See you again, sport,' said Porthos' master and I didn't know if he was talking to me or Marc but it sounded good either way. And it was. An afternoon in the river with Porthos was the best work-out a dog could want. One time we saved a man's life. Newfies do it all the time, you know. Porthos told me all about his heroes, the Sea Rescue team down at les Saintes-Maries in the Camargue. He'd watched them on a Show Day and picked up some techniques. 'The sea teddy-bears,' they called them. Can you imagine! A bit like having a 'fluffy firemen' day! But they're good, believe me. First you've got to have the swimming skills and the strength but then the knack is in the teeth. You've got to grip the right bit in the right way. If it's a Human drowning, then the wrist is the bit to hang onto. 'When we were with our masters, Porthos showed me where the wrist was. 'Not too tight or you'll break the skin and that counts as biting, but not too loose either or you'll lose him. And then there's objects that Humans might be on top of, like boats or floats - if your teeth so much as touch an inflatable - pzow! bits of rubber everywhere and screaming Human to deal with. No, you've got to find something you can grip…'

So when we saw a man in a boat adrift on the river, holding some sort of stick with string on it, jerking his arm back and forward in a plea for help, we were on the case so fast the Teddy-bears Rescue Team would have begged us to join. With all his experience, Porthos went straight for the painter and I followed his lead, finding enough room further along the rope to get my teeth round it too. We both locked jaws round the painter for all we were worth and started towing the boat safely to the shore. The man was still shocked from his near-death experience and was shouting and waving the stick in the air. He'd been there so long that there was even a fish trapped on the end of his string but, with all the waving around, the fish soon wriggled free. We battled against the current, which runs deep and cold in some parts of the river, eddying round hidden boulders or submerged tree trunks. The boat was heavy and my jaws were aching by the time we got the man safely to the bank, where our masters were waiting anxiously.

'These your dogs?' The man shouted, his voice hoarse from the terrifying experience. We didn't wait to hear his thanks and our masters' pride in us. Like true heroes, we barked, 'Think nothing of it,' and charged off to go back in the river further along. 'Time dry is time wasted,' was one of Porthos' favourite maxims.

'Get him out of here and clean him up! He's filthy and wet!' was the greeting we usually received when we got home after a river afternoon. 'That means 'Hi, did you have a good time?'' Marc whispered to me as he toweled me dry.

The wind grew colder, the trees barer and the river was out of bounds for the season - on-lead walks there only and we stopped meeting up with Porthos. Marc was wearing more and more outdoor clothing, warming his hands in the coat pockets I'd eaten through six months ago to eliminate the middle-man in getting some treats.

Then, one evening, the sky dropped on our head. It had been strange all day, blocking light instead of reflecting it, heavy, 'gray' according to Marc. We were walking towards the hall for training class when the sky bombed us with white rain that tickled my fur and burst in icy drops on my nose and tongue. I left my tongue hanging out to taste some more. The flakes whipped around faster and faster as the wind caught them and soon the street was dancing in white spots, lamp-posts curving madly as they flickered in and out of swirls. Marc had a sparkling moustache already, as if he'd been dipped in ice-cream, and smells were disappearing, underneath a numbing cold freshness, purer than water, an absence. I whined.

'I don't like it either boy. It's heavy and it's drifting and I don't fancy walking back in an hour... for the sake of what, anyway. Let's just go home, shall we?' I couldn't have agreed with him more. Don't get me wrong - I loved the cold - but there was something wrong in the feel of it that evening. Or perhaps it had nothing to do with the snowstorm. Perhaps Marc already knew what he would find when he returned home.

Sometimes silence is worse than 'He's filthy, get him cleaned up.' Especially when there's silence where you don't expect it and two voices where you'd expect silence - the bedroom. I knew Christine was with Things to Do because she'd told us so but I hadn't realized that Things to Do was much the same height as Marc, smelled more of soap and could leave a house very quickly. Marc and I slept in the living room that night.

I will always remember the next day-break because it was dazzling white. I pawed to get outside to find out what was going on and my legs sank straight away up to my knees in wet cold white. Patou's first snow! What water is to a Newfie, snow is to a patou. I rolled in it till I was tingling. I bounded in it, feeling ten times as heavy as usual with each leap. I jumped straight into a roll-landing on ground that was soft as a bed (I'd managed to climb up once or twice to test the bed out but Marc and Christine had strongly discouraged this so I'd left bed-training until they were older). Marc had put wellies on and come out to see what I was doing, so I rushed him and rolled him in the snow. He laughed, a little weakly, but he did laugh. And he rolled the snow into balls. 'Still too powdery,' he said but he threw them high in the air anyway for me to stand underneath as they came down and explode them on my nose or in my mouth. Even now, snow is all the excitement of puppyhood rolled into one great explosive ball of fun. At the first flake I could fight ten wolves, fifteen stray dogs, mate with three young bitches and still have enough energy to sit and stay for two minutes. In theory of course. But that first time, even snow couldn't distract Marc for long.

A new atmosphere took over our home and went on and on, through the cold days, colder still with polite thank-yous during an attempt at a Christmas truce, while I chewed paper and got sticky tape on my fur. The truce lapsed again as the snowdrops came up. After the snowdrops, the freesias, then the daffodils and still no better at home. Christine and Marc would both shout then a silence would spread from where they were to poison every nook and cranny and it always reached me, wherever I hid. I inspected the house with my nose and peed in some key places, including against the bed, which still smelled of Things to Do, but it didn't improve the ambience or cheer me up. I chewed the stairs again as that had always relieved stress when I was little but the effect had worn off. I carried on chewing anyway. I chewed on my own paws until I'd worn small patches of skin pink. But they didn't notice.

'It's Mother's Day,' Marc pointed out. 'Funny now I think of it but I had been wondering ... before... whether you might want to start a family...' he laughed, the sort of laugh he gave these days, that sent splinters through my head and started me chewing, my tail this time.

'You care more about that bloody animal than you do for me so what chance would a baby have?' Christine had the last word that time and slammed the door as she left the room. Pleasing as it was to have Christine confirm my rank, that didn't make up for the tensions in the pack. I couldn't pull the two of them together, which showed weaknesses in my leadership.

If only things could go back as they were, to the days when the three of us would snuggle on the couch together. I remembered Marc throwing a stick for me and they both smiled when I fetched it and took it back to Christine. I wanted them both to smile again. So, if a stick was what it took, I'd find a stick. I whined and pawed the outside door to go into the garden. Marc opened the door without a word, his shoulders drooping.

A dog with a mission, I quartered the garden but there was nothing, absolutely nothing. I sat and scratched behind my left ear to help me think and looked around above ground level. A ray of sunshine illuminated the answer. Of course, it would mean some serious digging but no patou was ever averse to some hard work in soft earth so I set to with enthusiasm. Perhaps a little too much enthusiasm. Within minutes, I'd uncovered the root system of my chosen stick, and a den wide in either direction. Now all I had to do was get it free of the wall and there was no way I needed the top bit so I stood on my hind legs and chewed through the stick at an appropriate height. Now this really was a stick. She was going to be ecstatic.

I could hardly get the stick through the door it was so big and the roots made it clumsy at one end, bashing bits of earth around the hall but I waddled down the hallway, past the kitchen where Marc sat with his head in his hands and, as these were exceptional circumstances, I pushed into the bedroom and laid the stick on the bed beside Christine. The result was even better than I'd hoped. She screamed, 'My wisteria!' and burst into tears. I'm sure you know as well as I do that women often cry from overwhelming pleasure but I really hadn't expected so much.

I was about to get Marc when he rushed into the bedroom of his own accord. He too was overwhelmed. 'Oh Izzie,' he said and he too burst into tears. Tactfully, I withdrew back to the garden, thinking they would make the most of their moment together and that perhaps I'd have more fun barking at the gate.

So I never will know what Marc did wrong but Christine left that very afternoon. And I moved onto Marc's bed that same night.

Chapter 7

We became seriously filthy. Without anyone saying, 'He's filthy!' I didn't get cleaned up, just brushed thoroughly once a week. Which was just perfect as far as I was concerned. Mother advised us to run away if ever our Humans threatened us with Shampoo as it would strip off all the oils that water-proofed our coat. A hose down with water was acceptable but not enjoyable so running away was still a good option. On the other hand, brushing was essential and a Soum de Gaia always stood still for grooming unless of course an incompetent Human hurt you, in which case clamping your teeth around her hand worked wonders - not actually biting of course, just pointing out that pain could go in two directions. I had trained Marc well as a groom. He would start at the bottom of whatever area he was working on, brushing out clumps and tangles at the ends first, then hum a little tune while he worked his way towards the root sections. He always worked along the direction the hair grew, lulling me half-asleep when he followed long sweeps along my back and haunches, until he was satisfied with his work. Then, he'd give a few strokes against the grain and finish off with a light massage with a rubber brush to remove any loose hairs. All very pleasurable. And after a week of splashing through puddles and rolling in anything that smelled interesting, I'd be willing to admit that my weekly brushing was a necessity. Marc never let me down but he was letting himself down, badly.

It's possible that he was still grooming himself weekly but if he was, it didn't show. His face was prickly against my tongue and his clothing was more and more rewarding to lick, salty and offering hints of egg or tomato sauce. 'I've got to sort myself out,' he told me. 'Everything's going to the dogs - no offence. Even the toilet's so miserable that it's stopped cleaning itself now she's gone.'

If everything was going to the dogs, then that meant me so I made the most of it. The bathroom door was permanently open so I went back to drinking from the toilet. As the toilet seat was always up, there were no complaints this time about the water sprayed all around. In fact, there were no complaints. I was now comfortably installed on the sofa beside Marc in the evening as well as on his bed for the night. I knew that a paw wasn't the same as a hand to hold but he'd get over her. He would start some new project. Perhaps something exciting would happen at that 'work' he went to every day. Little did I know.

I'd grown so used to being left alone that I could hardly be bothered chewing a bit of carpet or wallpaper. If I did, it was more for old times' sake than for any real frisson. So I was a bit surprised when Marc came home, saw I'd torn just a teeny strip of wallpaper - and he tore a strip off me! I hadn't been told off since Christine left. And for something so trivial! I didn't understand it at all. And then he repaired the torn wallpaper! I just wasn't in the mood to start the game again so I left it alone. I couldn't work out what was going on. Marc was coming home from work and, after our walk, cleaning the house. He vacuumed, dusted, washed surfaces. He did some touching up on paintwork. He threw away the piles of newspapers and washed up the nine mugs that were all over the house, growing mould in coffee dregs (even I found the contents a bit off-putting). He cut our walk short, using words that filled me with dread, 'Have to stop there today, boy. Things to do.' He didn't even seem to remember Christine's Things To Do.

Then he came home from work for an hour, sometimes in the morning, sometimes afternoon, 'to show people round.' It reminded me of the Choosing when I was a pup. Even the voice Marc used was the same as our Human had used with the Choosers. Surely he wouldn't sell me? Of course not. I put such an unthinkable idea out of my mind and made the most of our pre-breakfast walks, our evenings together and whole weekends of shared activities.

A man and a woman were 'shown round' twice. Then three times. Then Marc spent an evening stroking me beside him on the couch. There were tears in his voice when he spoke to me. 'I'm sorry, old son. I know you don't understand a word I'm saying but you've been my best friend and I'm going to miss you. But I've thought about it all and it just won't work, taking you to live in an apartment. I've got to sell the house anyway, to give Christine her share, and then this promotion came up, Paris. It's a big chance for me. I've got to get on with my life. But it wouldn't be fair on you to take you with me. You'll be better off with Jean-Pierre and Beryle. There's no point drawing things out. It's only going to be harder.' Who for? I wondered, my head fuzzy with incomprehension.

The doorbell rang. Marc let in a loud jolly voice and a sweet, low one. 'Oh the darling,' said the sweet, low one, stroking me under the chin just where I like it.

'The kids will love him,' said large jolly voice.

'I'll come and get you when I've got sorted out,' Marc told me. 'I promise.' He clipped the lead to my collar and gave me away.

That was the start of the parallel universe. Everything was like what I knew but different. And I mean everything.

'Get in the car, boy,' loud jolly told me, and there was an open car boot, so I jumped in. But that wasn't how it was supposed to go. It should have been Marc's voice, saying, 'Hup' and 'Good boy' and the boot should have been lower and more homely, emitting old smells of wet dog - me - not aerosol gases and artificial orange. I stuck my nose to the window to see where we were going but it steamed up so quickly I could just see flashes of houses, lamp-posts, cars, houses, lamp-posts, cars.

And then front door, hallway, doors into a kitchen, a sitting-room. I knew what they all were and recognised none of them. My ears were on full alert so when Jean-Pierre shouted, I jumped backwards, starting a metallic clang from the radiator that caught me in the back.

'Hey, kids we're home!' Jean-Pierre yelled up the stairs. His name, like everything else, tasted alien. Then there was noise everywhere, whooping and running down stairs and arms waving. I had nowhere to go so all I could do was lay my ears back and let my fur speak for me. It couldn't have been more erect if twenty bears had turned pack and were charging at me, and I was just about to growl at them all to quieten down a bit and stay still, when Beryle did it for me.

'Calm down now! It's all new to him and he's bound to be a bit nervous so just take things slowly.'

' Woooah, he's huge! Can we stroke him?' Before there was an answer, hands waved over my head like snakes and I had to duck so as to avoid them. If they didn't get the message, I'd have to give a warning air-click with my teeth.

'I don't like the look of that,' commented Jean-Pierre. 'I thought he was supposed to be friendly and good with kids.'

'Give him time. Let him sniff your hand first, underneath his nose not above it. Then if he's happy, stroke underneath his chin…'

'How can I tell if he's happy?'

'If he's happy, he stays still, looks a bit more relaxed. Watch, like this.' And once again, Beryle moved her hand gently towards me, let me sniff lavender and cinnamon, and then she stroked under my chin, calming me, so I hardly noticed the two squeaky ones putting their hands on me at the same time.

'Let Sirius settle down for a while till he gets used to us.' The pack moved towards the sitting-room so I followed and turned round and round in the doorway to make myself comfortable for a long sleep, somewhere I could keep half an eye out for trouble.

'No, not there Sirius.' A big hand grabbed my collar and stopped me lying down. I was too tired and confused to complain so I allowed myself to be dragged into a corner. 'That's your place.' I closed my eyes, drifting into a world of endless puppyhood, sitting between Marc and Christine on a sofa that turned into swift river currents, Newfie barking 'swim with the current, patou, don't waste your strength crossing it till you have to.' I could feel little fingers curling into my fur from time to time but it was Christine and Marc so that was all right and I let myself drift far away. Newfie would rescue me if the current was too strong.

Gradually, the strangenesses became ordinary. Food smelled as usual but it was difficult to relax and eat when the squeaky voices were jumping around and shouting. They moved so quickly that I was tempted to play with them, a little game of chase and catch their arms in my mouth, like I used to do with Marc. Then they flapped a lot, which was exciting so I'd firm up my hold a bit and give a little shake. They liked that and squeaked louder, but, 'That's too rough, Sirius,' Beryle kept telling me. 'Boys, Sirius didn't mean to hurt you. He's just learning what he's allowed to do here.'

She was wrong. I'd learned pretty quickly what I was allowed to do. Absolutely nothing. Lying in doorways? No. Sitting on the couch? No. Bedroom? Absolutely forbidden, as were several other rooms. Digging? No. Playing? No. In fact, I hadn't yet worked out anything that was fun, that I was allowed to do. And 'No' usually meant a big hand grabbing the back of my collar. 'You have to be firm with a dog, especially one this size.' I really didn't like my collar being grabbed and I'd tried to tell Jean-Pierre that I preferred to be asked politely. When I felt the yank on the collar, I'd turn my head, very sharply towards his hand, just warning him, but he never took the hint.

Essentials like sleep and food were permitted, in the prescribed places. Jean-Pierre took me out on the lead each day and, from the lamp-posts and verges, I worked out who my neighbours were. I could tell what their Humans had been eating from the dustbin scents, and if Jean-Pierre allowed me a sniff-stop, I knew where the rats and squirrels had crossed our path. All this was as it should be but it was as if there was a silent machine at the other end of the lead. Jean-Pierre was an enigma. He didn't talk to me, he rarely touched me - apart from hauling on my collar.

Our walk always went the same way and the same distance, past two streets north, past four streets west, past one street south and then past five east, back to the house. I still couldn't call it home. Sometimes on these walks, we'd meet someone he knew and then I'd hear Jean-Pierre speaking.

'Beautiful dog you've got there.' A strange hand would dive onto my head and I'd duck. Or someone I'd met a few times would do the same and I'd accept that. Or someone more polite would offer a hand to sniff and follow up with a caress along the side of my face.

'A bit dominant,' Jean-Pierre would say. 'But nothing I can't handle. You just have to wait till they show you proper respect before you reward them with affection. Wife and kids are a bit soppy with him but I keep the balance. Fantastic pedigree. His father's a champion.' And then they'd have a chat about their families, or work or fishing. I wasn't well-enough behaved to be taken fishing, I'd heard Jean-Pierre telling Beryle.

And so my life plodded on. I passed whole stretches between nightfalls without telling myself that Marc had promised he'd be back. My tail wagged when I saw Beryle smile at me. She sneaked me little bits of cheese or saucisson and gave them to me if I'd sit for her. She told me that Jean-Pierre worked too hard, had lots of worries and that when he was on holiday he was a different man. This different man took her out for meals, kissed her a lot, played with his children, wore shorts. But I just had to take her word for it as there was no way they were taking me on holiday. I'd heard Jean-Pierre telling Beryle that.

I let Gilles and Fred chase me around the garden and tried not to knock them over when I changed direction. I wasn't scared any more of them whooping while they ran, or of their little hands diving into my fur. Sometimes we sat together, and I felt the old warmth of the puppy-pile flooding me as their skinny little bodies flanked mine. If Gilles was there on his own, he'd tell me about school, how he liked English but got stuck in Maths, and how he'd have to work on his Maths because he wanted to be a doctor. And if Fred was there on his own, he'd tell me about how his big brother was the most important thing in his life, how he didn't think he'd manage when Gilles went up to big school and he was left to fight his own battles. And I'd listen and wonder what it really meant, being a brother.

All in all, I was starting to belong, when it happened. I had two feeding-times, early and late. Early was peaceful, just me and Beryle, and I could relax. Late was like eating in the middle of a wolf-attack. Gilles and Fred were just home from school, charging around the kitchen, grabbing biscuits or crisps or some cheese out of the fridge, passing behind me, beside me, pushing each other and shouting. Beryle was shouting back at them to get them to behave and the stress was buzzing in my head like a hornet. Usually, Jean-Pierre was still at work but on this occasion he had come home early, right into kitchen chaos, where I was trying to swallow the second half of my bowl of food.

His voice boomed over the others. 'Stop that racket, all of you.' Beryle turned red, probably from stopping in mid-shout. Gilles let go of Fred, who lost his balance, grabbed at a chair and kept falling. His half-eaten sandwich fell straight into my dog bowl where I was concentrating on eating and I snapped at the unexpected treat as it arrived in mid-air, followed a second later by Fred's hand as he kept falling and stretched towards my bowl to break his fall. Fred shrieked, whether because he was shocked by falling or whether because he saw my teeth snapping near his hand, I'll never know. He started to cry and Beryl pulled him up, sat down herself, pulled him onto her lap and comforted him. Jean-Pierre was glaring at me. I turned back to the remaining food, a pleasant aftertaste of bread and cheese lingering in my mouth.

'That is it!' the voice boomed. 'If anything, he's becoming more aggressive!' I felt sorry for Gilles as it was only the sort of brotherly spat that would be forgotten in five minutes when the two of them would be building Playmobil cities together.

'But Jean-Pierre…' Beryle began. Fred was choking on his tears, crying because he was crying and couldn't stop, not because he wanted to. A bruise was already starting on his knee.

'You've been too soft with him from the start - I did warn you! Two months now and he's getting worse!' Beryle cuddled Fred closer. 'And I'm not having a threat to my child staying in this house a moment longer!' I looked at Gilles, wondering when he too was going to burst into tears. His face was ashen.

'Dad, Izzie didn't mean it,' he whispered. And my heart broke as I heard my real name at the same time as I understood. I was the aggressive one. I would have to go. Even then, I thought Fred would sort it out, or Beryle. Fred sobbed louder. Beryle opened her mouth.

'I've never seen him do that before.'

'You would say that, wouldn't you! Well even if it's true, it's once too many.' Look, I begged them with my eyes, cheese sandwich, not a mark on Fred, not a mark. I would never. But I knew from the taste turning sour in my mouth that there was no trace of cheese sandwich. I knew how slow Human perceptions were. Perhaps even Fred thought I'd meant to bite him.

'No, Beryle. You saw that programme on TV. A dog that will bite someone who touches his food is dangerous and I'm not having a dangerous dog round my children. Another little accident like that and Fred might not be so lucky.' The lucky individual was still crumpled and bemused on his mother's lap, his shoulders heaving, his lip trembling.

'What are you going to with him?' Beryle asked, her voice quieter and quieter. I could hear the hum of the fridge.

'The only responsible thing. I'll take him to the S.P.A. refuge.'

'No!' screamed Gilles. 'You can't get rid of Izzie!'

'One day you'll understand, son.'

'I hate you!' Gilles rushed from the room and his feet thumped two stairs at a time up to the slam of his bedroom door.

'We promised Marc,' Beryle said.

'Not to take on an aggressive dog, we didn't. And he's

moved to another life, no chance of him taking the dog back, so it would be cruel to even tell him. No we've got to do the responsible thing, however hard it is.' Jean-Pierre tousled the hair of his younger son. 'The dog will be well looked-after and they'll find an owner with no children, who can give him the discipline he needs - no soppiness.' His gaze made it clear where the soppiness had come from. Beryle returned the gaze, hard-eyed, her arms tightening round her son. 'I'm sure Daddy's right,' she lied, 'Izzie will find someone who loves him as much as we do and can look after him better.'

And so, after some collar-dragging, I found myself left at the S.P.A.. Sirius of the Soum de Gaia, aggressive dog, not to be trusted with children.

Chapter 8

The outlook was limited. Unless you liked concrete, fencing and dozens of dogs. One of whom was staring up aggressively at my knee-caps, unable to crick his neck enough to meet my eyes.

'What are you in here for?' he demanded. Terrier fur covered a long short body that said 'dachshund' but his pricked ears and pointed muzzle suggested a soupçon of German Shepherd.

I wasn't really in the mood for discussing racial backgrounds and I had a strong feeling that being a Soum de Gaia didn't count for much among the inmates here, even if it might help spring me in the extremely unlikely situation that Marc didn't find me quickly. How exactly he was going to find me was another of those questions that I buried as deep as ever the black Kong toy went in the rose bed.

'It's a mistake,' I told the Dachs-terrier.

His eyes stayed hard. 'That's what they all say, so you might as well own up.' A black, middle-sized pure mongrel charged back from the bars, where he'd had his nose poked through, right by two of the Humans. He was still panting as he gasped, 'Child molester,' and six pairs of canine eyes levelled on me, as high as they could reach.

It was the kind of silence that raised my hackles and laid my ears back, ready for attack. None of them were more than middling size and the one-eared whippet was little more than an extra number but the black mongrel and two labrador types, female, were well-muscled, the Dachs-terrier didn't look like he'd back down easily, and I would really rather not feel the bulldog's teeth on me, anywhere. She was the one who spoke.

'Bitten three of the little horrors now,' she declared.

'Maisie's our top scorer against kids,' I was informed. 'She's hoping to hang onto her record and you being a big boy and all, we were wondering.... how many?'

'One,' I said, 'but I didn't.'

There was a marginal shift towards happy in the wrinkles on Maisie's face. 'Three,' she confirmed, 'in three different families. Hate them, the way they dart around like rabbits, and shriek and pull you about.'

'And the really little ones always smell of food, then the moment you chew a bit of stale breakfast off their bib, the Mother's shrieking like you'd eaten the baby.' Wrinkling his wire-haired face, Dachs-terrier reflected. 'Anyone eaten a baby?' Negative responses. 'No, I suppose not. It's one of those crimes that get talked about and just don't happen,' he said, almost wistfully. He turned back to me. 'They keep sending Maisie off to a family,' he explained, 'because she's so cute, there's always someone choosing her, and all they want is one less mouth to feed so they don't mention the fact that Maisie isn't what you'd call good with children...'

'I'm very good with them,' Maisie contradicted. 'Sort them out in under twenty-four hours even with parental surveillance.'

'... and then she's back in here with us till the next sucker turns up.'

'Good old Maisie,' came the chorus from the labradors and Maisie flexed her wrinkles to their cutest.

'I like children,' objected the black mongrel.

'You're just an old softie, Prince,' Dachs-terrier told him, wuffing under his breath to me, 'six years old so no chance of a family, too old, and we all know what that means. He can forget his retirement plans.'

'Hey, boys and girls, grub's on its way.' A wave of barking had started out of sight and reached the pen beside ours, where another group of three or four dogs were pressed against the wire at the path-side, ears alert and tails starting to wag.

'You're in luck, big boy. It's the princess,' Dachs-terrier wuffed. 'Just smell that.' We all inhaled, deeply, breathing in young sweat, the salt tinged with sweet female scent. Vanilla and hot, clean hair. Shoe polish over dried mud from the river I'd played in with Newfie. She smelled of smiles.

We could hear the clanging of the cage door and glimpse Human clothes, jeans, a bucket swinging amid the eager press of hungry hounds. Her voice, purring. 'Now then you lot, no pushing, no shoving, no stealing each other's food. Hey, Jack, how are you today? Clementine, well hello, you.' She had a word for everyone in turn, by name and the cages where she had been already were quiet, transmitting sleepy dog vibrations, even some of the sighs and snores that come from a full tummy when all's right with the world. The same calm descended next door, we upped our volume and it was our turn. The cage door rattled and in came the one they called Princess.

'Hold on now, Jack. And Melba, just hold on a minute.' She put her bucket down on the concrete floor, gently pushed away Dachs-terrier and a labrador who were investigating a quicker route to food than seemed on offer. The bucket was covered and the Princess crouched beside it and looked me straight in the eyes, her arms held out towards me. I stood stock-still and looked back at her. She had the most undoggy eyes I've ever seen. I could see all different coloured rings but don't ask me to distinguish the colours - I'm not Human! Hazel, I heard someone say, later. You can count on two paws the Humans I've looked long in the eye; make it four paws to include dogs, followed of course by a serious knockabout so my memories of the dogs' eyes are somewhat blurred by the subsequent gnashing of teeth. I'd seen eyes full of love, eyes hard and angry, tired eyes, guilty eyes - but never eyes like these. It was as if the river and the Newfie and my master on the bank had all been distilled into two little pools of fun and friendship. I couldn't look away.

'So you're the little new boy,' purred the voice. 'You don't look so bad. We never get the full story, you know. Sometimes you're made out worse, sometimes better, sometimes it just depends on who you're with… people can be so stupid with dogs, so ignorant.' As if aware that her voice was becoming harsher, she shifted position and resumed, purring again. 'So little boy, Sirius, are you going to say hello? Come and see me little boy, Sirius…' she kept looking at me as if she was trying to read something in my face. I still couldn't move but I couldn't look away either and I wanted to hear her talk to me again. The purr was reaching right down to my double dewclaws and I liked it. I liked it a lot. She laughed aloud. 'Izzie,' she said. 'Izzie, come and have a cuddle little Izzie.' The princess towed me into her eyes, steady as the Newfie against the fastest river current, and I was saved, her fingers running through my fur.

The door clanged behind her when she left. I'd been given my own food bowl, and the Princess made sure we'd finished eating, without stealing or scrapping, before she picked up her bucket and moved on to the next pen, leaving a hypnotic calm behind her.

'They're not all like that,' Maisie pointed out, her eyes gradually de-glazing.

'No-one's like that,' said Prince.

'What is she in for?' I asked.

'Poor innocent!' Maisie rolled on her back laughing, but not for long enough to let anyone take advantage and try a quick dominance challenge. I had the feelng that Maisie was a match for most dogs and I wouldn't want to face her in a no-holds-barred session. I avoided thinking about three children.

'Storytime at dusk, everyone, and we'll get Sirius here up to speed. But for now, let's have some peace and quiet.' Dachs-terrier, Jack, stretched out on his back, and was soon cycling his back legs in dream-chase. His confidence in leaving himself so vulnerable made me feel secure, even amongst these strangers, but I wasn't ready to open up that far and I hugged the side of the cage, protecting one flank, just in case. I kept an eye on the others from time to time, taking turns as to which sleepy eye I flicked open, but gradually sleep took me, shredding the stress of the day into dream cushion-foam.

Twilight, the violet hour, when your eyes turn wolf, ready for the night hunt - or ready to prevent the night hunt as you guard your flock on the mountain beneath the stars. A Soum de Gaia doesn't need to be taught to protect; the instinct is deep in our blood along with the courage to fight bears, wolves and wild dogs. Twilight is the call of the wild to the wild, the unleashing of the inner wolf to the ancient battleground of dog eat dog. The great protectors of Soum de Gaia legends, Cesar, Achilles, Boudicca, had all been able to tap their inner wolf - and control it. 'Rip out an enemy throat and lick a friend's,' was the protector's maxim, according to Mother. Her brother worked the mountainside and had prepared from puppyhood, learning from *his* aunties, uncles and Human. 'The difference between great protectors and good protectors is a matter of seconds; great protectors can switch from enemy mode (rip throat out) to friends (lick) in one movement. And the dog that takes too long to switch is doomed, whichever way he gets it wrong. And you must feel the bond that gives you strength, the bond that links you with your flock, so that you will protect them with your dying breath.'

This Soum de Gaia woke to twilight, sheepless, penned myself. I could see the start of night-shine in the others' eyes and some restless pacing told its own story of inner wolves. 'Storytime!' The howl came from a pen down-wind of me so I had no idea who started the call but it was taken up all round the compound until Jack barked, 'Newcomer first,' and the silence of listening dogs invited me to begin.

Between dark and light, between wolf and dog, I howled my tale to the unseen voices that echoed mine as they lived my life with me. We sang the mountains and my brothers, my Choosing and my Undoing.

'It isn't fair!' my voice belled out.

'It isn't fair!' sang out around me.

'I didn't do anything wrong!'

'He didn't do anything wrong,' the pack agreed.

'And Marc will come for me!' I howled. 'He promised.'

'He will come!' the voices echoed, reaching for the crescent moon that glowed in a darkening sky.

'He will come,' I was hoarse as I finished the big story of such a little life. 'He will come.'

Jack nudged my leg. 'Sleep now, little brother. We keep watch over you.' He barked an ending to the twilight. 'The dark has risen. Until tomorrow, my friends.'

'Until tomorrow,' rose the chorus and then I dropped into a sleep deeper and blacker than under-river.

And so the new pattern of my days took shape. I found out that the Princess was only one of the Humans who brought our food and the time dragged longer and longer between her visits as I looked forward to them more and more. One non-feeding time, she turned up with a collar and lead. 'Now then Izzie,' she said, crouching and holding out her arms, as she had the first time, 'I want to know a bit about you to help me find you a home, because you're just beautiful aren't you. Look at those big brown eyes of yours.' She was purring again and it was just the same as before - there I was, with a chain fastened round my neck and the lead in the Princess' hand. I didn't have to be shown an open cage door twice - I was out of there! I'd like to say I felt guilty about leaving Jack, Prince and the others languishing in the pen but I was all nose, sniffing dog, dog and different dog, followed by strange petro-chemicals, then overpowering Human sewage that blasted my nose out of action until I cleared it with some sneezing and coughing. I'd been towing the Princess along nicely, mostly on my right but criss-crossing if something interested me, when a sudden jerk on my neck halted me. I looked back but she was still smiling so that was all right. She just hadn't been properly lead-trained. So I started off again at a good pace, to show her how it went. Ow! Jerk again.

'You really haven't been trained to walk nicely, have you,' she said. Funny, but that was just what I'd been thinking. I figured we'd get there, between us, and wagged my tail to encourage her. You won't believe this but the poor girl was all over the place, and amazingly rough at times for such a slim thing. I'd get her walking nicely and then she'd suddenly veer off to the right, giving such a yank, I'd have to follow her. Worse, she'd sometimes veer left, tripping me up as she crossed me. Didn't she know that was bad manners? And she made it clear that she wanted to be on my right *all* the time - I call that downright fussy to the point of compulsive. Or we'd be trotting along nicely and she'd stop, when there was no smell of any interest at all, and then when I'd really caught hold of a good scent and dug my heels in, she wanted me to walk straight on! No sense to it whatsoever.

After a while, I got fed up getting jerked around and wondered if I could second-guess her for more fun. So I really concentrated and the minute that I could feel a leg muscle turning, well I was turning before she was - no jerks, there. And I could feel the stop so with my muscles on red alert, there I was, a dead stop - no jerks there. And seeing as she had this obsession about being on the right, I bounded along on the left and sniffed left of her. And sniffed her, up close beside her hip, and then something wonderful happened. Her hand brushed against the side of my face and she told me what a superstar I was. I wanted more of that and tried again. Right up close, face stroked. Now this was more like it. But then there was a strong scent of fox and I just had to work on this a bit more so I stopped and braced myself firmly. Glory be! She stopped too! So it seemed she could stop with me sometimes she liked to be the one who decided. It certainly wasn't what I was used to but I had a straight choice; do what the Princess wanted and get compliments and caresses, or try to take the lead - in every sense! - and get unpleasant jerks spoiling my walk. Well, which would you choose? The truth is, that once I let the Princess take control on walks, I enjoyed them even more. She made all the decisions and I could relax and concentrate on pleasures of the nose.

Sometimes the Princess would appear with the lead and take one of the others out, often Maisie, and I would hate whoever had gone in my place, filled to biting-point with envy that built up and built up in the long wait imagining someone else's pleasure. When my rival came back in through the cage door, I swear I was poised to sink my teeth in her - or him - and enjoy it, but then the Princess would name each of us in turn, a word, a caress, and you knew that everything in the world was how it should be and you had your rightful place in that world so you didn't need to fight about it.

And when it was my turn, I wouldn't even glance at the poor suckers left behind; it was my turn! I'd come to know the usual route, the tow-path by the canal, the waste-ground where the Princess lost all sense of direction and zig-zagged in different ways each time and I was so used to reading her movements that I could turn with her and listen to what she was telling me at the same time.

'I suppose I ought to introduce myself,' she said one day, as we were sniffing otter by the canal. 'Elodie Jouve, eighteen-year old failure in mid-crisis. I know I can't do well enough in exams to be a vet, I don't see myself working in a dog's home, all swilling out cages and dishing out food, with no time for giving the walks and training you really need... good boy, that's nicely done...' hand against cheek, warm silk against deep fur. 'Now I'm just a volunteer I can take you out for a walk like this but if it was my proper job I wouldn't be allowed, I'd have too many boring jobs to do. And then my parents keep trying to tell me that I should grow out of this thing about dogs...you really are a quick learner aren't you, that's my Izzie, well done...but it's what I'm good at, I know I am. I suppose we'd better go back now, back to our cages. Well done, Izzie!'

Sometimes, as I said, it wasn't the Princess who fed us. In fact, sometimes we were hardly fed at all. Sourface gave out a tenth of the food the Princess did.

'Takes it for her dogs at home,' Prince told me. 'Heard her telling her man about it when he came in his car to collect her and they walked around to look at us so she could show off her favourites.'

'Who's her favourites?'

'Not us. Or we'd get fed.'

'And Bigwoman allows it?'

'Maybe she knows and maybe she doesn't. She steals money.' I never had seen the point of money but you can't be around Humans very long before you work out that it's important to them. I had cost 'a lot of money' to buy. I had caused 'thousands of euros worth of damage.' 'A fortune' had gone on my vet's bills. Marc told me that he had paid 'a high price' for loving me but he never said how many euros. The S.P.A. people thought I was worth 'a lot of money' and might 'get something back' for them. I thought perhaps they'd lost a dog of their own and could use any profits I made them to find this other dog. There was some good in everyone, a Soum de Gaia learned at his mother's teat. But I knew that it was not good for a leader to be stealing money.

'If she's the leader, then isn't she stealing from herself?' I asked.

'It's not her that people give the money to, it's us.'

'But we can't use it.'

'I tried eating money once,' said Jack, 'don't know what they smell in it.'

'I know what you mean,' a labrador joined in. 'The coins are even worse than the paper. Break your teeth on them.'

'That's beside the point. As I was saying, Bigwoman keeps two books and she writes all the money that people give her in one book, then only some of it in another book, so that she can take some for herself.'

'Where does the money come from?'

'When people die, they like us to wag our tails and remember them so they give money to spend on something to make us happy and wag our tails.'

'Like food.'

'That's it.'

'Do you know their names?'

'No idea.'

'So how do you remember them?'

'If we're being polite, we say it before we eat. 'Thank you all the people we're remembering for giving us the food we eat.' We say it in our heads of course, not out loud, otherwise the Humans would take our food away because we're too noisy. And we never say it, even in our heads, with Sourface because if you don't eat as quickly as possible, she takes it all away even if you're quiet.'

'Is there nobody who works here and actually likes us?' I wondered.

They consulted each other. 'Beanie-hat's not so bad. He's just a bit sloppy when he has personal problems. And he hasn't had time to become like the others. Bigwoman says it gets you down after a while and there's no point to it. She says she was like the Princess once.' We contemplated the impossible.

'Like Maisie could have liked children if things had been different,' I offered.

'Exactly,' said Maisie. 'I didn't like children and things aren't different so that proves Bigwoman couldn't have been like the Princess, not ever.'

I didn't like the thought either but I couldn't help thinking. 'And if Bigwoman was once like the Princess, then the Princess could turn into Bigwoman.' They all looked at me, horrified.

'Where do you get your ideas from, little boy!' Jack snapped at me. 'Anyone can see they're different breeds; just look at their eyes and the way they stand, no to mention their size.' He dismissed the absurdity. 'But as for anyone who likes us… Sourface says there's no gratitude. She says she's found homes for dogs and then they don't behave themselves so they get brought straight back. And she's disgusted by the illnesses.'

'That's something else there's no money for - vets. And least of all for preventing illnesses. You can forget the little routine trips you used to make. If they find a family for you, that pays, you might get cleaned up, but otherwise, forget it. Noticed you're itching have you?' I'd started to scratch while Jack was talking about illnesses and now I could feel the little tracks parting my fur, itching. When I scratched, hard enough to draw spots of red on my claws, the itch just moved somewhere else; it didn't go.

'Fleas,' Jack told me, 'and that's just the beginning. Soon you'll be wishing all your problems were fleas.'

Chapter 9

As leader of the newcomer's compound, Jack organised the twilight story-telling, our in-mates having their turn first. No-one seemed to mind the fact they were hearing the same stories over and over. If anything, it added to the resonance of the echoes.

'We were happy with our family,' barked Melba.

'There was glitter and paper and ribbons,' added Clementine.

'Cuddles, walks and a soft bed specially for us in a warm corner.'

'A family with big children, who took us for walks and talked to us.'

'At first.'

'Then we had less cuddles, less walks, more time shut away.'

'Our drinking water wasn't changed every day, sometimes not for many days and sometimes they forgot to feed us.'

'We were forgotten,' howled Clementine.

'They were forgotten,' we echoed.

'We had no master any more.'

'We had dark corners and each other.'

'We grew. We weren't cute. They said so.'

'They took us out in the car. We thought they loved us again. The car was full of suitcases, bags and hats. We thought we were going for a walk with our family.'

'They tied us to a signpost where cars were parked, at the beginning of a huge road where cars and more cars zoomed past.'

'They left us there. We thought they'd come back.'

'But we got tired waiting.'

'We got thirsty and when the sun moved in the sky it beat down full on us and we got dizzy. We felt sick.'

'Then a woman got out of a car. She said, 'You poor things. I wish I could keep you all.' She gave us water in a plastic cup and put us in her car. She brought us here. She said, 'They'll look after you.' We get food. We get water.'

'We want a family,' howled Melba.

'We want to stay together.'

'They want a family. They want to stay together,' we told the indifferent moon. The sisters lay down side by side, licked each other's muzzles and waited for the whippet, Éclair, to tell her tale.

'I was a champion,' she barked. 'Chased the rabbit for my master, round the ring with men shouting my name and yelling numbers. My master called me a goldmine.'

'She was a goldmine,' we celebrated.

'Then I got slower. My master called me old and useless. He took the big carving knife, the one he used to jab into a loaf of bread to eat at lunchtime and he held my head down on the kitchen table. I thought he was going to give me tablets or special food to make me run faster. He always held my head still when he gave me tablets. He cut my ear off, the ear with the tattoo on it. He threw my ear in the bin with the potato peelings. He swore at the blood on the table and kicked me. Then he drove me into the woods and left me. I tried to go home to my master, to tell him that I wouldn't displease him any more, that I would try and run faster.'

'She tried to go home to her master,' we howled.

'But I couldn't find the way. I held my head on one side because my ear burned. My ear dripped iron-smell on the fallen leaves. I went round the woods. I grew hungry. I chewed on trees. I ate the grass. I drank the streams and puddles. But I couldn't find my way home. I stayed alive but I felt weak. I forgot how a dog behaves. I copied the birds and the squirrels but I missed my master. I was too hungry to sleep, My belly was eating me, burning all the time, as if the pain in my ear had moved into my stomach instead. Then a man came. I thought it was my master and I wagged my tail. He stroked me, He said, 'What bastard did this to you?' He was angry and I wet myself but then he was gentle again so I wagged my tail, hoping he wouldn't get angry any more. 'You must've been here months, old girl. You've worn your teeth away, eating bark.' He looked after me till I was better but he said he couldn't be my master. He brought me here. He will find a family for me.'

'He will find a family,' we insisted, and Éclair joined us in one last howl, sitting, throwing her head back so that the ragged edge to her left ear was silhouetted against the moonlight.

Then Prince stood. 'From puppyhood to dog, I grew up with the two babies in my family. I made them smile by licking their feet when they were tiny and my master and mistress stopped them pulling my ears or poking my eyes when they were old enough to experiment on objects. My masters loved me, looked after me, walked me and the children together. We were one family. First Linda, then little Alice started school and every day my mistress and I would walk to meet them. I loved the sound of the children coming from the playground. And the sound of my master coming home from work. And the daytime with my mistress. She sang while she cleaned the house, cooked some food. She took me shopping with her or to visit friends. I can keep myself warm through the winter on my memories of my family. I am lucky.'

'He is lucky,' we howled.

'They died. They went out in the car and they didn't take me. They said, 'Bye, Prince, see you soon.' And they didn't come back. There was an accident. The police said so when they came to my house where I was waiting for my family to come home. One said, 'He's a bit old.' The other said, 'No, he's not old at all and he's sweet. Give him a chance. He'd make a lovely family pet.' And they brought me here. I will always love my family.'

'He will always love his family,' we echoed.

'I can love another family too. My heart is big enough.'

'He can love another family too.'

'My new family will come.'

'His new family will come.' As Prince lay down, Maisie was standing up and I could swear she licked his face as she moved past him but as the clouds drifted past the moon, it could just have been a trick of the light. There was no trace of softness in her deep wrinkles as she gave voice.

'My family was three; my master, my mistress and me. They often carried me places. I looked down on the world and saw that it was good. I gave my approval to those beneath me. They sat me on their laps in cafés, on the train one time. Life was comfortable. Except for one very bad problem.'

'Life was comfortable,' we shared with the clouds obscuring the moon.

'Each morning my mistress went to work and I was left in the garden. I watched through the gate, learning about the world, sharing my views with passers-by. The same people went past every day in a hurry, then it would go quiet and I would lie in the garden, watching the butterflies and the bees. I was happy.'

'She was happy,' we howled.

'There were three big children who went past me early every day, with heavy bags on their backs. At first we just barked at each other and they flapped their arms. They shouted and made fun of me and I barked louder. Then one of them brought stones and hurled them through the gate. I was hit and it hurt. The next day one of them climbed onto the gate and threw bigger stones down at me. The gate was too high for me to reach the child and bite his legs that dangled over my territory but I tried, jumping and barking a warning. This excited more shouting and stone-throwing. The garden was small and I had nowhere to run away. Every day, I was hit by more stones as their aim got better. I loved Sunday.'

'She loved Sunday'.

'I loved Sunday anyway because my master and mistress didn't go to work. But also the children didn't go past.

My mistress had been getting very fat and smelling different for a long long time. She told me she was having a baby. The house changed. She went away and came back with a baby. He frightened me with his crying and sick-milk smells and the master and mistress told me how frightening he was. They said, 'There, there Maisie, there's nothing to be afraid of,' which is what they said in thunderstorms or when the sky filled with a red billowing ball that hissed and carried people in a basket. That's how I knew the baby was a menace.

People came round to see us. To see the baby. Some of them remembered me and stroked me too. I liked that. One of the people was one of the stone-throwing children. I saw his legs dangling over the edge of the sofa, swinging backwards and forwards. He stuck his tongue out at me when no-one else was looking. He wasn't high on a gate out of my reach. I sank my teeth in his leg and he screamed. I did the bulldog grip and bits of his leg came off in my teeth when they finally made me let go.

'She's not safe with the baby,' my master said. My mistress

cried. My master cried. They brought me here. And I don't regret biting children. They ask for it.'

'She doesn't regret biting children. They deserve it,' we howled. Maisie stayed, defying the night sky, long after Jack had taken up position. The listening silence deepened. The other dogs knew what they were going to hear and I could sense their mental preparation.

'Imagine,' boomed Jack, 'imagine a Human with no love. A Human who has been given no love and who only knows how to give hurt to others. A man who gets pleasure only from giving hurt. This man was my master when I was a puppy.'

There was no echo.

'Shut your eyes, my brothers and sisters, know your own body, the connection between claws, feet and pads, the leg joints, ribs, skin, muscle... move your tail, feel how it sways, how good it feels.' His voice mesmerised us. I could sense every tiny part of my body as he described it, separately and as part of the living entity that was me. 'Every part of you that you sense can feel.... can feel *pain!*' His voice snapped my eyes open as if I'd been whipped.

'I was a little puppy of twelve weeks old and I was tortured,' howled Jack, 'by Human hands, Human feet and whatever objects a twisted Human mind could imagine using. Someone suspected. Someone told the Animal Protection Agency. They came to get me. They said that I was lucky, that there was nothing wrong physically that wouldn't mend, that I'd only have a few scars.'

Not one voice howled that he was lucky.

'They said my Master might even go to prison. They brought me here. Humans can't be trusted.'

'Humans can't be trusted,' we wailed softly.

'I will not let anyone Choose me. I will not place faith in a Human ever again. I will accept the caress of the Princess and her kind but trust in Humans is dead.'

'Trust is dead,' we whimpered.

'I am with my family here. You are my family and I will never leave here. I will speak for the newcomers, I will speak for the old, I will fight against corruption so the food gets shared and we minimise disease. I will even help those who want families and I will not bite your Choosers but no-one, no-one will be allowed to Choose me. I will lead the storytelling until my story is over. You are my family and I will stay here.'

'We are your family,' bayed a hundred voices at full power, splintering the night.

A shutter slammed in the distance and we heard a Human voice dim in the distance, 'Don't know what's up with them tonight. Just listen to that racket.'

'We are his family,' we answered the Human. 'We are his family.'

'And Marc will come,' I whimpered to myself before a sleep marred by looming shapes, which slipped away from my snapping jaws only to swoop down on me from another direction.

Chapter 10

Basic hygiene was difficult with seven of us in the small concrete compound that served as our indoor and sleeping quarters, walled on three sides with a grill door set in the part wall, part fencing on the fourth side. There was an area of decking against the wall opposite the door, big enough that four of five of us could pile onto it if we were feeling extra-friendly. Being a weatherproof kind of dog, who couldn't bear being too hot, I took the concrete option and let the others sort themselves out. You wouldn't believe how sensitive and warmth-loving a whippet is. Even on the hot summer nights we get here in the south, Éclair shivered at night unless she was flanked by hairy company - or one of the blankets that got dropped off every now and then by two helpers. Of course the blankets helped keep the fleas warm and happy too but Jack was right - I'd got used to the little crawlers who used my body as a pile of blankets on a bed, with supper thrown in.

I reckon that the indoor area was about four times my length by about three times, if I lay down and stretched out, with a bit extra for some decking, so you can imagine that seven of us, none small, had to accept some serious invasion of personal space. Inevitably, tempers frayed at times and Éclair was safest to take them out on, so we did. Luckily, she was lightning quick in submission and none of us had that evil streak that leads a dog to follow through with punishment after the recipient's shown a proper humility.

The best we could manage for a little space was to go through the opening in the back wall into the 'exercise yard' when the others were sleeping indoors, or vice versa. 'Exercise yard'! Don't make me laugh. It was the same size as the sleeping quarters. The only difference was that there was no decking and only one wall. The rest was all grill fencing so we could see out front, where visiting Humans sometimes walked round and waggled their fingers through the mesh, like pale sausages. More often though, the Humans would stay the other side, lingering round the door where we would shove and jostle to get a look at them, just for some entertainment and something to talk about. I was big enough to see through the fencing above the wall beside the door, if I stood on my back legs, but there was no purchase on the wall on our side so I couldn't keep it up for long. And my view there was obscured by squares of white paper, seven of them, which the visitors stared at, saying 'Oh the poor thing' and 'What a pity he's so old' and 'I'd rather have a puppy.'

And if you weren't actually on the decking, whether you were indoors or outdoors the concrete floor was always wet. Our Humans hosed it down daily, after they'd cleaned up into a bucket whatever of our droppings hadn't been recycled by my less discriminating cell-mates. I can't pretend I didn't join in sometimes. I was so often hungry. And even when the Princess had fed us, so we'd had enough to eat, there was always the feeling that something was missing. The food just didn't leave us satisfied the way it should have done. So if there was extra protein going, even if it was brown and recently dumped by a friend, 'Waste not, want not' we all said.

'Don't know why we bother giving them food at all!' Bigwoman said. 'It would save us money if we just put the contents of this bucket straight back into their bowls.'

'She wouldn't!' breathed Jack. 'Would she?' But no, not even Bigwoman went that far in economies. And one of them would hose down the pen daily, without fail. There was no chance of the floor drying as the ceiling of the indoor part kept it permanently in shade and the outdoor pen was overshadowed by the other buildings crowding round. But as Jack said, 'Pneumonia's less certain than heat-stroke.' Those who slept on the decking dried out, especially Éclair and the others with smooth coats, but my underbelly and flanks were permanently brown and damp. I wasn't confident enough to stretch out on my back to sleep, so it was always the underbelly against the concrete when I was lying down - and there wasn't much else to do after you'd walked the ten steps each way round our two compounds. Although, when I lay down, it was becoming more and more difficult to get comfortable, with the itching over my body that had grown worse as damp hair clogged up during the process of shedding.

I forced myself to a regular 'tour' of this kind, as slowly as I could manage, and at every step I filled my head with the memory of Marc's garden, of racing along the hedge to bark at the cyclists, or dusk patrol along the boundaries to keep the wolves at bay. To make my 'walk' last longer, I called up a garden boundary memory for every chain link in the fence.

'Hey, big boy, you're turning into a pacer - you don't want to do that,' Jack warned me. 'You start doing that same old round-the-cage every day and before you know it, you'll be putting your paw across your nose exactly two steps after you pass the door going anti-clockwise, every single time you do the self-same route. That way madness lies, my friend. I've seen it before.'

And so I had to vary my exercise. I'd do four steps and turn to go round the other way. But it was hard not to fall into whatever new routine I'd set up and let it take over so that my body was repeating, repeating, repeating…and my heart howled for a mountain-side covered in snow, to bound and free my cramped soul. I stopped myself remembering my garden, I stopped myself imagining the mountain. I could no longer cope with the idea that there was anything other than this cage so I wrapped up my hopes and memories and buried them with my love for Marc, to be dug up again when the time was right.

Visiting times were a distraction. Humans would walk past, pointing as we crowded round the door to take a look. Once we heard the wave of excitement among the pens before ours on the visitors' route and then a smiling lady reached us, holding out ham sandwiches. 'They were left over and I thought you'd like them,' she told us, breaking bits off and making sure each of us had a bit.

But the only times I stopped worrying for my sanity were when the Princess took me out. Then my nose came alive, I could feel the spring in my legs and I overdosed on thinking. I wasn't the only one.

'I've been thinking,' Elodie told me. 'I can get some money for vocational development, perhaps work as a vet's assistant and find someone I can shadow, learn to become a dog trainer. That's what I really want. There are training classes here on Thursdays so I'm going to go along and start with that. You're gorgeous, aren't you. You did that so well, Izzie.' It was amazing how good her judgement was about everything and if she wanted to be Queen of France, that was all right by me, so vet's assistant? Dog-trainer? No problem. I panted my agreement happily.

The more important my walks with Elodie, the harder it was to walk through that chain-link door back into the pen. On this particular occasion, for some reason, perhaps a hawk screeching above me, or even a rain-drop hitting my head - I can't remember now - but I looked up while Elodie was opening the door and I saw a photo of myself with a text underneath. A Visitor stopped and read it aloud, 'Sirius, Pyrenean Mountain Dog. I am only 17 months old, a cuddly teddy bear, with an excellent pedigree, looking for a loving family.' it is a shock to see yourself up for Choosing and to hear the words Humans use about you, especially when they put them into your mouth. I thought back to my puppyhood Choosing and to what had changed.

The words from the paper had that same false tone. My image was still 'cute' and it was still good for business that I was a Soum de Gaia, even if the Humans here didn't know enough about our line of aristocrats and show winners to talk the way my Soum de Gaia Human could. But that was just a detail. There was some big difference but I couldn't put my paw on it. What was it that was so different this time? Not that I wanted to be Chosen you understand, as I was only waiting till Marc came, but I started to brood about it, particularly as I listened to the comments of Visitors in the afternoons. I heard some of what I expected when they looked at me. 'Cute', yes, 'teddy bear', yes, 'huge', of course. So what was wrong with me? Why did people walk past quickly? 'There's something in his eyes,' I heard one of them say.

I pondered this 'Jack,' I asked, 'can you see something in my eyes?'

'Why? Do they itch? Are they sore?'

'No.'

'Well there's nothing in them then.'

'But a Human said there was.'

'Ah. Well Humans are always seeing things, aren't they. Probably something to do with colours.'

'But that wouldn't be something *in* my eyes.'

'Yes it would. There'd be... brown for instance, in your eyes. And you know they've got all these colour words. I tell you, they see differences.' I wasn't convinced but until I got a better answer, it would have to do. I determined to read the notices on our pen, and on the other ones, and every time I went out with Elodie, I managed to add one more description to my store.

Humans seemed to like reading about bad things happening to dogs, so the dogs who'd been tortured had long stories. I talked to some of the dogs in the other pens, a quick word in passing, and I found out that the worse the story was, the more 'Ah, the poor thing' comments and the more likely the dog was to be Chosen, unless it was Old of course. And Old got younger every year, according to those who'd been here a while. 'Probably about five years now, is old.'

'Why do Humans prefer to choose dogs with really bad stories? Instead of the dogs who are happy and healthy?' I asked Jack.

'As far as I can work out, it makes them, the Humans, feel good.' This made no sense at all and my expression said so. Jack persevered. 'Suppose you had to choose between a master that was bleeding and smelled of death, and one that was strong and healthy. Which one would you choose?'

That was obvious. 'The strong and healthy one.'

'Right. Well, Humans have a big flaw in their genetics. They call it pity. And when they feel pity their brains turn to mush like when you smell a female on heat and you can't think straight, only they have it all upside-down and think pity is good. So they think it is part of being a good person to choose the one that is bleeding and smells of death, even if it means leaving the other one to a horrible fate.'

'But that's stupid.'

'And they feel like they are very good Humans if they think they are doing a big rescue.'

'What about Humans who choose a happy, healthy puppy that lives with his mother, perhaps a Soum de Gaia just for example, and they promise to love it forever, and they do give it a good home and they do love it forever? Aren't they good Humans? And then no-one would come here in the first place…'

Jack had to think about this. 'Not to other Humans, 'he decided. 'Not nearly as good as Humans who Choose a dog here. And the really good Humans are those who Choose a dog with a really bad history.'

'So why don't the Humans here make up really bad stories for all of us? And what about the Humans who bring back their Chosen ones and Choose again? Are they good or bad?'

'You ask too many questions Sirius. I have no idea. You keep expecting Humans to make sense and they just don't. Work it all out for yourself.' We'd both been aware of Clementine recycling some scarcely dry droppings but I didn't expect Jack to run at her, barking like a Human. 'No, Clementine!'

Startled, she dropped a half-eaten treat.

'Look at it!' Jack barked at her, and we all looked. And saw small white worms wriggling. 'You got worms, girl. And eating them back up isn't going to make you feel good.' Clementine didn't need telling twice and our Human complained that the poop bucket was filled to overflowing these days. She didn't seem to notice the worms though.

I remembered Marc crushing up tablets, lots when I was little, then summer and winter only, and putting them in some fromage frais for me. 'A little treat for you, boy,' he'd say, 'Here's your de-wormer.' And it was a treat too, silky smooth in your mouth, that farm smell that reminded me of puppyhood and the freshness of first tastings 'You've got some white spots on your nose,' he'd laugh and then wipe my nose with a bit of kitchen towel (if Christine was around) or with his hand, which he then wiped on his trousers (if Christine wasn't around). But I didn't know what worms were or did. So I asked Jack.

'Hazard of communal living, big boy. They get passed on from dog to dog, droppings and lickings. Then they live in your guts, eat your food, make you thin, or false-fat, extra hungry or sick and tired. They wear you down, sap your strength, make you ill all the time but they don't kill you.' He gave a sharp cynical bark. 'Wouldn't be good for parasites if they actually killed you. Torture inside, I call it.'

'Does that mean we've all got them?' I asked quietly. I was all right because I'd been given a tablet not long before I came in.

'Perhaps. Probably.'

'Will they give us tablets?'

'Probably. Perhaps. But not till it's their time to give tablets and that's never often enough with new dogs coming in and re-infections all the time. And tablets get rid of the worms you have *already* got, they don't *stop* you getting them! Tablet today and worms tomorrow - quite likely in here.' My tail had never been as low and I slunk off to lie as far from other dogs as was physically possible. Waiting for Marc was hard.

I kept wondering what was so wrong with my piece of paper on the fence. Surely I didn't want it to say I'd been abused and tortured. Did I? It was only when Elodie changed my notice that I finally worked it out. 'There,' she said. 'I've written a much better one for you, little boy.' It was the first time I'd been out for a walk with her that I was actually keen to get back to the pen so I could check out the new paper.

She stopped at the pen door and read the paper aloud to me, proud of herself. Below the photo it started off, 'Sirius, Pyrenean Mountain Dog, excellent pedigree.'

'I'm going to track down your pedigree name, Sirius, and find your Breeder.' There was a bitter note in her voice that I hadn't heard before. 'The people who work here say there's no point because even if they do, the Breeders never help. I don't see how they can know that if they don't try. And they're always too busy here to do anything anyway. Oh I shouldn't say it like that. They really *are* too busy here. It's just… they don't seem to care any more.'

No, I wasn't bothered about my pedigree name not being there although I did wonder if my Soum de Gaia Human would find Marc for me. I read on. 'If you look in my eyes, you will see the sadness people have given me, the people I loved who have left me here and I will need time to love and trust a new family.' Was that what was in my eyes? 'I am very well trained, don't pull on the lead, know all the basic commands and will be a loving companion for a family with patience and plenty of space for a big dog.' There was nothing to say that I bit children but there was nothing to say I didn't. Perhaps Elodie hadn't been told. My Princess had put her paw exactly on what had been missing though, the difference between this cuddly teddy bear and the baby one of the last Choosing. This time, I had a history. This time, I had all my experiences, good and bad, and anyone who lived with me would have to live with my past too. Which would be fine because Marc would come.

Chapter 11

'Sometimes I think you're the only one who understands me,' Elodie told me, as we meandered along the grassy canal banks. I sniffed rabbit, water-rats and joggers' sweat still lingering in the air. 'The only one I can talk to. My parents are nagging me to get a proper job and stop fooling around with animals. They think I'm going to grow out of it but why should I? It's as if there's being a vet or there's being a little girl who likes animals. That's how they see it anyway. And now my only idea has gone all wrong. And Xavier hardly knows I exist. He's friendly enough but that's not what I want. How do you make someone love you, Izzie?' She kicked a tuft of grass and I nuzzled up against her side. She stopped and put her arms round me, burying her face in my fur, her words muffled. 'If only you knew, boy, eh? Well I love you, you know.' She stood up again and laughed, then fished a hair out of her mouth and spat to clear it.

'Look at the pair of us. If only I was older, had some money, a place of my own, I'd take you like a shot Izzie.' She stopped again, without me feeling any jerk on the lead, I was so used to reading her body and following her movements. She looked right into my eyes and I looked right back, battling the instinct to look away; that was something else she was teaching me but I wasn't totally comfortable with it yet. It just didn't seem polite to me to make eye contact with someone you weren't trying to challenge but she kept telling me what a good boy I was, so it was obviously fine by her. 'Izzie, I'm going to make you a promise.' Her face was all straight lines, a hint of what she was going to look like in ten years' time. 'If I get myself sorted, have somewhere for you, I'll come back to get you.' She tossed her hair back and laughed, a brittle sound.

'What am I saying. My mother's right. I can't even look after myself never mind a big beautiful boy like you. Oh, Izzie, it's all gone wrong. But I can't go to the class again and there's no way I'd learn anything from brutes like that. It started OK, with one trainer taking the class and another there to learn and help, an assistant I suppose. And I was thinking, 'That will be me, I can start as the assistant, then take a class myself.' And in my head I was working out what to say to people to get them doing leadwork properly, like I've been doing with you, my little superstar.

I looked at the different dogs there - they were all really big apart from one dachshund and that was the first thing I didn't like. Now, you know perfectly well that I make fun of the little dogs we pass, and call them your breakfast, or a pair of gloves, but that's not the same as being horrible in public and picking on the one small dog all the time. The trainer was saying things like, 'You with the furry- teacosy' and 'the rugrat', 'Are you sure it's training he needs not platform-soles,' and 'if you get him mad does he burst out of his little suit and turn into a green rottweiler.' He thought it was so funny and all of it was just pretty stupid really.

The woman with the dachshund took it really well, just smiled as if it was good fun, but you could see she felt uncomfortable. Some of the others were embarrassed but nobody had the guts to say anything. That's me too. I wish I'd said something. How is it that afterwards you always think of these really witty things to say. And the trainer was a big bloke so you could see he thought big blokes had big dogs, the macho thing, and little wimps and women had little dogs. And this dachshund looked at his mistress, so full of love, so keen to obey her, you just knew he could have been the star of the class with any half-decent trainer.

Then there was some of the usual walking round, orders and so on, but none of it done with respect and, I'm not bragging now Izzie, just telling the truth, I could have done it so much better. I'd have given them advice about leads to start with. Can you imagine, a full-grown rottweiler in a harness! Anyway, things got worse. The second rottweiler there was lunging at other dogs, a snap here, a snap there, all in the air because the master had him strung so tight on the lead he was choking and couldn't actually get near another dog. The trainer said nothing about the way the master was tensing up the dog and just carried on as if everything was fine.

Then, the trainer wanted some work on ignoring other dogs and just walking past so at this stage they were all going to criss-cross. The woman with the dachshund was a bit nervous and asked if it was safe, meaning with the way this one rottweiler was growling at the others. 'Don't you worry, love, I don't think your little killer will cause too much damage,' was the reply so people laughed and it would have been difficult for anyone not to join in. Then off they went again and, of course, it was bound to happen. The aggressive rott lunged and snapped, pulling his master off-balance, He picked on a German Shepherd that wasn't going to take it lying down and answered straight back, and the rott just turned furious and took a chunk out of the dachshund's leg. So there were about four dogs getting into a fight, their masters pulling them off each other, kicking and hitting them, and what do you think the trainer did? Screamed his head off, joined in the kicking and hitting, then - I still can't believe it -

he went round the dogs that were being calmed down by their masters and he clouted each of them across the head! He yelled, 'Teach your dogs a lesson they won't forget so they never do that again!' He didn't go near the aggressive rott though - told the master he'd need a muzzle on his dog for next time and that he should 'sort his dog out'. As if that wasn't what the class was supposed to be for.

The dachshund had already gone - his mistress was rushing him off to the vet. I'm sure he'll be all right physically but what do you think he'll feel about other dogs now? And do you know what that bastard called after them? 'He's too small to mix with the big boys - you'd best find a puppy class somewhere'. No apology, nothing! And even the people there just carried on - they didn't do criss-cross again but they used the walking in a circle exercises. The closest I heard to a complaint was one man saying he wasn't going back because it might suit German Shepherds but his dog was a cross and he didn't see the need for hitting like that. Well it doesn't suit German Shepherds either, Izzie, and I'm not going back ever!

I'm just going to have to start all over again. Maybe find a proper Breeder, with a kennels, do a qualification in dog care, become a pet beautician! I just don't know.' The walk was over too quickly, as always, and we were heading back to my pen when we bumped into Sourface.

'I thought you were going to wash out Pen 4!'

'I felt like a walk,' replied Elodie.

'You felt like a walk,' Sourface mimicked, putting her hands on her hips. 'Well I feel like a holiday in the Maldives but we don't get what we feel like, us, we have work to do!'

'It's good for the dogs to get out.' Elodie wasn't backing down and I could smell the burning resentment in Sourface as it caught fire and turned her face red.

'Don't you tell me what's good for dogs! Coming here with all your fancy airs and graces. Everything you know comes from books! And doesn't include muck, which is what the real work is my girl. Mucking out. Day in and bloody day out. Not traipsing round the countryside.' Two bitches, neither backing down, spelled trouble that could be a fight to the death. I nudged the Princess but this was not the day for her to be diplomatic.

'Well while you're mucking out, perhaps you can put some flea powder down and get some sprays or flea collars. These dogs you know so much about are scratching themselves to ribbons and all it would take would be a little preventive treatment...'

'Fleas? Fleas are nothing! Shows how much you know. Don't suppose you've thought of what your friend there is bringing back from your country walks together. If he hasn't got infested with ticks, he'll have grass spikelets and when you're enjoying yourself all week, the ticks'll give him piroplasmosis and he'll be ill for the rest of his life - if he lives - and the spikelets will stick in his leg or his back and burrow their way God knows where to infect his throat so he chokes or make a weeping hole in whatever part of his body they end up!' I started scratching myself. There were really some things I'd rather not know about. Sourface seemed to have won the face-off though. More's the pity.

'I'll brush and check him before I go,' Elodie said in a tight little voice and motioned me to walk on with her.

But Sourface never knew when to stop. 'And apart from the time we haven't got, with dogs coming in and going out every day, where do you think the money's coming from for all this treatment you want us doing? Just tell me that then?'

Unfortunately, Elodie did. She whirled back round and yelled, 'If some people emptied their own pockets of what shouldn't be in them, there'd be plenty of money! Come on, Izzie,' and without another word she stalked towards my pen, opened the door and entered, ignoring the shout behind her,

'What do you mean by that? Come back here and explain what you mean!'

'Oh Izzie, what's going to become of us?' Elodie pulled a brush and scissors out of her rucksack and started the long job of working through my knots and tangles. She cut off piles of greasy hair, sighed a lot when she saw the pink itchy patches on my flanks and she sprayed these with something that stung a bit but left a pleasant cool numbness behind. I felt her tears dropping on the patches of bare skin, like the spray but with love added. 'This was supposed to be special,' she told me, 'the first time I've groomed you. And the first time you've been groomed since God knows how long. The cow! No ticks, no spikelets and that will get rid of the fleas for a bit anyway. I just wish I could help everyone.' She packed her bag up again, looked wistfully around at all the dogs wagging their tails. 'See you soon,' she told us, she told me. Yet another Human promise to one more gullible dog.

'That looks bad.' Jack flicked Éclair's ear back into place and the whippet instinctively raised a back leg to scratch the offending part, already crusted with dried blood from previous scratching.

'It's driving me crazy. I can feel these... things... crawling round down inside my ear. If I could bite it off, I would - I'd have a matching pair then.' No-one laughed. 'At least the other ear's safe!'

'Ear-mites,' Jack confirmed. 'Thought as much. I can lick the surface clean but I can't do anything about what's going on deeper down...' He turned to me. 'Lots of the dogs with floppy ears have black mud in their ears... itchy and irritating but you can live with it. Not with mites though.'

Éclair bashed her head against the chain-link fencing and

whimpered, 'What am I going to do?'

'When the Human comes, make it obvious to her. Put your head on one side, whine, scratch behind your ear, show you're in pain. You've got to see a vet.'

It was Sourface who came with the food-bucket and we made sure she had a clear view of Éclair. I'd been keeping my distance anyway, my own lop ears itching with imaginary ants at the very idea of catching mites. Éclair followed Jack's advice to the letter, pawing at Sourface to get her attention, then whining, scratching, shaking her head - the whole works.

Sourface put the bucket down again wearily. 'There's always something wrong with you lot, isn't there. I swear you do it on purpose. I suppose I'd better get Madame Clunier.' She picked up her bucket and carried on with feeding the dogs in the next pen, and the one after that. We listened to the routine noises of hungry dogs anticipating food, then quietening, in the usual wave of sound that indicated the feeding route round the centre and we waited. Finally we heard the voices of Bigwoman and Sourface coming our way.

'... too many dogs. Not surprising they're spreading disease and there's just nothing I can do to prevent it. New one coming in, that has to be kept on its own, and we're just running out of space. We've left it long enough, Lea, sentimental fools that we are. We'll just have to make a selection...' I never would understand people. I would never have believed that Bigwoman and Sourface would Choose some of us to go their homes and be their pets. I wasn't sure that was necessarily better than being in the pen with the others, however cramped things were, but at least it showed that they cared.

'I agree completely. And the other thing we've left too long is this question of volunteers.'

'Yes, I've been thinking about that, too. I'm not sure it's worth all the paperwork we have to do. When we have an

Inspection, that's all they go on about, 'insurance for volunteers, suitable training for volunteers, what tasks do they carry out, information about the dogs… on and on.'

'They take up my time with all their questions and for every job they do, I have to check up on them and put things right. They overfeed the dogs, fuss them too much and wind them up, waste time taking them for walks when they could be washing down the pens. And I don't trust what they say to other people….'

'What do you mean?' Bigwoman's voice was sharp.

'I've heard confidential things about the centre being spoken about in the street.'

'Like what?"

'All kinds of things. How we canvas for money and who's made donations. Rumours about the finances here…'

'Indeed. Well we'll see about that. Thank you for letting me know, Lea.'

'You know I will always work for the good of the centre, Madame Clunier.' Sourface was simpering now as she opened the door into our pen and the two women came in, eyes only for Éclair, who was whining and holding her head askew.

Bigwoman bent over Éclair and, without any roughness, folded back her one ear. She inspected it for a few seconds, then shook her head. Then she looked at the fur alongside Éclair's flank. She pounced and squashed a flea between her index finger and her thumb, to a little smear of black and red. She shook her head again and sighed.

'You never can tell, Lea. The way that dog was behaving, you'd have thought there was a problem with her ear but that's so clean you'd think it had been polished.' Jack barked frantically and put his paws up, scrabbling against Bigwoman's legs. 'No, you get down. So the ear's fine. And we're looking at a strong reaction to fleas - you can see she's been scratching - that's what the blood is from, and she's clearly upset. Typical whippet, over-sensitive. Because of what happened to her, I suspect she has some sort of neurotic reaction to have a go at her remaining ear, whatever's wrong with her. Psychological problems, the poor thing.'

'She's got ear-mites, you stupid woman,' Jack barked frantically, so stressed he started chasing his tail in a circle.

'At least that's easily solved,' Bigwoman continued as she opened the door for Sourface to go through. 'Flea powder all the dogs in the pen, throw out the blanket, they don't need it in summer anyway, and buy a flea collar for the whippet, just to make sure. That should sort it out.'

Sourface carried out her orders as efficiently as if she'd always thought it a good idea to get rid of our fleas. It seemed strange not to have the permanent flicker of insect life pursuing its microscopic life along the forest trails of my body hair. We were grateful for the relief. But we had to listen to Éclair whining, becoming more and more incoherent from lack of sleep and pain. 'Voices in my head,' I heard her whimper. Jack made it his business to lick her ear clean as far as he could until the time came when she told him, 'No, it hurts too much, I can't bear for it to be touched any more,' and he slumped down beside her, talking to her in the lucid moments that became rarer and rarer. Sometimes you could see pus oozing from her ear and the smell of rancid flesh grew stronger but Jack never left her side.

'Drama queen!' laughed Sourface at feeding time, watching Éclair's crazed attempts to deaden the pain. 'You're not catching me like that twice!'

We looked forward to storytelling that night even more than usual - something, anything to take our minds off Éclair.

At last. 'Storytime!' the chorus raced round the pens and once more Jack barked his order, 'Newcomer first!' and we all stilled, waiting.

A voice as deep as thunder echoing round the mountains

tolled, 'I was born under skies so blue they dazzle, where the snow's so white the glitter bursts against your closed eyelids, where the mountains dance in the winter sunshine, dance all year round. I was born in the Pyrenees, with my two sisters and four brothers.'

One name ripped from my throat in a roar. 'Stratos!'

'Stratos' howled the pack. 'Stratos!' we greeted my brother.

'Why does he have to be alone in a pen? Why is he here?' I growled desperately to Prince, the source of all gossip.

Jack silenced me with a look and barked, 'Let us hear the story of Stratos.'

Chapter 12

'My brothers and sisters were a disappointment to me,' Stratos began, endearing as ever, 'too easy to knock over, too ready to submit. I was a strong puppy and I wanted to develop my muscles and reflexes to the perfection I imagined my father to be. All I knew of my father was what my mother told me and that filled my imagination with a proud male, the one I wanted to grow up to be.' The scent of Stratos' urine wafted down-wind to me. How had I not recognised it sooner, the acrid tang, salty, like mine but stronger, more concentrated, grass-killing. 'I copied the adult moves, the sideways pounce to catch a dog unawares and take it straight into a submission roll, the grip to the death on a tail…' my own tail swung nervously, 'and my own favourite, the ear-hold. I tend to attack from the right, lunge for the right ear and then I can lead my catch wherever I want, clockwise in a circle, straight to a Human, or down to hit the ground on his back.

But these were just the play of puppyhood with weak companions. I was always waiting for someone stronger, more of a challenge. On the day of my Choosing, I knew I'd found him. He was tall as a house, his eyes sent fiery sparks and forbade me to look into them. When I looked away, polite little pup that I was, he said, 'Good boy' and his voice was a volcano, a rumble with the threat of eruption always there.' This wasn't quite how I'd remembered Stratos' Human but I suppose we see our stories differently and it was strangely alienating to be a bit part in Stratos' story, about to disappear from it. We grow used to being the centre of our own stories and the earth shifts to reveal the abyss, non-being, death, when we disappear from someone else's story, not even missed. Still, if only for the sake of my reminiscing muscles, I was glad we'd moved on from tales of our shared puppyhood.

'He swung me up into the air so that my feet touched nothing but clouds and I was scared. And I wanted to please him and be called 'Good dog'. And my inner wolf wanted to grow up and fight him. To fight well, and to lose, to a real master. He put me down on the ground again and where his fingers touched me, stroking me, I felt the root of each hair follicle connect to his body. I was *his* dog and I was charged up with belonging. When he, Denis, passed me to his Female, Nina, I felt warm towards the whole world and I curled up like the little baby I still was and slept in her arms. It is good to be loved.

'It is good to be loved,' we howled.

'Even the strongest dog that ever lived needs to be loved. And needs to be mastered.'

'Loved and mastered,' we echoed.

'I knew nothing about houses, room, furniture... you remember what it was like to miss your mother, your brothers and your sisters, to find not one familiar smell, nowhere that you can settle because everything is new. You are full of curiosity and exhausted by so much to take in. You remember?'

'We remember.'

'Denis went somewhere and I heard a door open. I was sniffing around a chair and had only just realised that it smelled of dog, very recent dog, when a rattle of barks alerted me seconds before a black and white terrier landed on me, ordering me to submit quickly or else. Even though I was well-mannered enough to acknowledge his greater age and roll on my back straight away, he nipped my legs fiercely. 'I'm the boss here and don't you forget it!' he was barking and by this time - you know how slow Humans are - Nina was shrieking 'Fredo!' and swotting at the terrier with a cushion and Denis had come back in from the other room, following the terrier but much more slowly. He speeded up now, shouting 'Fredo! No!' and the shock ran right through me as his big hand welted the terrier's head. This was the first time I'd seen a Human hit a dog. I was very pleased about it at the time. Fredo whimpered, 'Sorry, master,' and let me go, but not without a snarled, 'See you later.'

Denis sent Fredo to lie in his place, a little basket beside the fire, where he glared at me throughout the evening, making me so nervous I couldn't sleep. 'That will sort Fredo out,' Denis told Nina. 'We just need to be firm with both of them.'

'Do you think they'll be all right together tonight? It is the puppy's first night here.'

'They'll be fine.'

The moment the kitchen door was shut on me and Fredo, he sank his teeth in my leg. 'And that's for getting me into trouble!' I was so scared I ran under the table, piddled in the corner straight away and sat there shaking. Fredo chased after me. 'And don't think you're sleeping there. That's my place!' I slunk out, passing him so quickly that his teeth snapped on air. He dragged the blanket out of its basket, put it on top of another one that had been laid out under the table, growled, 'Shut it and let me sleep. Just don't come near me.'

The next morning, Nina said, 'Fredo took both blankets last night - and he slept in the place I'd made ready for the pup. Because he's going to grow so big, I didn't think a basket would suit him. What should we do?'

Denis laughed. 'We don't need to do anything. Boys will be boys. They'll get used to each other - it's natural that there's a bit of sorting out to do at first. And I'll make sure they respect us, don't you worry. Just be firm with them. Your Mum dropping the kids back here after school?'

'Uh-huh.'

And so began my new life. I met the young Humans. They were playful and we would chase round the garden, bat paws or jump on each other, as young animals do. Unless Fredo came outside and spoiled the game. He would ignore the children and target me with his spiteful nips, marking me closely and dive-bombing me whenever I tried to play. The children would squeal, 'Leave him alone Fredo,' but they would be afraid to play with me after that. Sometimes, Denis would notice, and then Fredo would be smacked, hard, but I'd learnt that a smack for Fredo meant bad news for me later on. The best times were when Fredo stayed indoors with Nina or when Fredo was asleep and hadn't noticed me stealing outside to play.

Denis was at work most of the time, sweating in his too-many-clothes, pulling at the tie round his neck the minute he walked through the door. I could hear his car coming home, five streets away Nina said, so Human in her amazement at our ordinary senses. I would be there waiting for him at the door, ready, to jump at his legs, lick his hands, wag my tail. And Fredo would appear, snapping at my tail, snapping at my haunches, enough to annoy me but not enough to earn him any blows. 'Enough of that, Fredo,' the Master would say sternly but his hand would make it a lie, stroking the little rat-catcher who was quick enough to wag his tail and lie on his back to mollify Denis.

And then would come the moment I waited for twice a day. Morning and evening, I got Denis to myself. Fredo 'didn't need walks, he got enough exercise in the garden'. Serve you right. I stared my thoughts at Fredo, who looked longingly at the door when he heard the cupboard opening and my lead being taken out. 'Not you, Fredo,' Denis would say, and I would glance at two hard marbles of hatred above a black nose.

We walked the same walk every day, morning and evening, but it never *was* the same walk to me. 'You don't get bored, do you,' Denis commented, plodding a little after a 'hard day' while I tracked every beetle, bin-bag and even badger that had crossed the road since last we walked round the block to the park. I was allowed a long lead, 'a bit of freedom because you're a pup' and I wanted nothing more than to be by my Master's side, share in his strength and his love while we sniffed the changes in the weather and the light, together. Full of curiosity, I rushed towards new objects of interest, people. Denis tugged me back, tugged me forward - I hardly noticed, I was all nose. If the bin-men had just been collecting, I was delirious. Rotting chicken, cotton wool with Human blood on it, fermenting milk dregs. How could Denis stay so calm and walk in a line, when every step was a new scent. I was young, I thought every scent was for the following.'

Oh, Stratos, my brother, we didn't know when we were young that the track is set and whatever scent we follow leaves the others unexplored, a tease and a memory. I wondered about the paths not taken, the choices that weren't ours to make.

The story continued. 'I learned to understand my master. He was afraid of puddles. If there was a puddle in my sleeping quarters, he grew angry, as we all do when we're scared, and he hit me, naturally - the weakest one is there for the leader to treat as he chooses - so I hid when he came in and there was a puddle. He was pleased with me for hiding, said it showed the right attitude, but he still hit me. The puddles stopped happening when I was bigger than Fredo so Denis had nothing to be afraid of any more, he didn't hit me, I didn't hide and he said I was a good dog.

He was a strong master. When he was pleased with me, he praised and caressed me. When he was angry, he shouted and hit me. I began to work out what was good and what was not allowed but I was very young and it was difficult to understand why I was hit for chewing, when my new teeth coming through drove me mad with raw throbbing. Or why I was hit for greeting my mistress with an enthusiastic leap and rolling her on the ground. Or for barking to protect my family from the dangers that passed our house daily. So I didn't do these things when my master was around. Sometimes he would show me marked furniture or a destroyed cushion and he would shout, 'You bad boy' and hit me but I had no idea why. I thought it was like the puddles, something annoyed him and he showed what a strong leader he was. He told me he hit me because it was good for me. I was toughening up and when he noticed that I no longer flinched or ducked while he hit me, he hit me harder.

I was a strong dog and wanted to be like my master. Of course I accepted anything from him but not from the others. Just like him, I didn't allow caresses all the time, only when I wanted - and then I would use my great paw to make my demand, If I didn't want to be stroked, I would walk away, or if I was lying down and couldn't be bothered to move, I would growl a little. They got the message. Nina told Denis, 'He's not the sweet puppy he used to be. He's getting …bossy… with me and the children.'

'That's because you're too soft with him,' Denis told her. 'Look at how he behaves with me - perfect. And if he respects me like that, everything is as it should be. He's that sort of age now too, finding his feet.'

'With feet that size, it shouldn't be a problem!'

'If it makes you feel any better, now he's seven months, he's old enough to be trained, so I'll work with him and you'll be able to tell him to sit, give you a paw, whatever you like.'

Nina smiled and kissed my master. 'That sounds great. I just wish I had some of your technique with dogs, that's all.'

'One master is enough, don't you worry.'

It must have been about this time that Denis saved my life. We were coming back from a walk and just before getting home, we passed a chocolate labrador with his master, who stood having a chat with someone else. The lab sent a little snap my way, with 'You think you're hard, do you, Fluffy?' and I lunged at him to protect my honour. Denis pulled me back hard, hit me and said, 'All testosterone at the moment,' then moved me on. I could hear the pride in his voice and I could hardly wait to make him prouder still. I aimed a growl behind me to show it wasn't over. If the lab's owner kept on chatting, and I was fast enough, I could finish the conversation from the sitting-room window, which looked out over exactly this spot in the street.

I was into the house and up the basement stairs as if a rabbit had flashed its tail at me and run ahead. I'd give him 'Fluffy!' I took a flying jump at the window barking threats and insults at the top of my voice and instead of bashing my face against the glass as usually happened, there was no resistance at all and I was travelling at full speed out onto the ledge between two open windows. Now this was what I call a dominant position! I was looking down on the lab from one storey up, hurling war-cries full-throated, foaming at the mouth and prancing. The labrador was turning into a pool of chocolate and I was building up to another frenzy when my foot slipped. I scrabbled at the ledge with my claws but I was heading inexorably into a much less dominant position one story lower, when the most almighty yank on neck nearly strangled me.

'Stratos!' screamed my master.'

While I listened to my brother's story, I couldn't help reflecting on what it meant with regard to Humans. This was another example of the type of human behaviour that I find puzzling. What did Denis think this might achieve when a dog was falling out of a window? We're not supposed to be good at recall at the best of times, us patous. Luckily he wasn't just shouting but, rather more practically, hauling on the lead that Stratos was still wearing.

'In my haste to defend my honour and that of all my household, I'd rushed ahead still wearing my lead. So Denis grabbed hold of the end and I was pulled backwards into the sitting-room with a throttling jerk that left me choking on what spit I hadn't deposited on the labrador and his owner. I like to think I covered them fairly thoroughly before my shaming exit from centre stage.

My master shut the windows. I waited to be hit - it wouldn't hurt me any more than the burning round my poor throat. Surprisingly, Denis shouted at Nina instead, for leaving the windows open, and she performed the correct submissive gestures so it all finished quite quickly.'

I knew exactly what Stratos meant. You'll notice that Human females use words a lot when showing submission, 'Sorry, I didn't think, I didn't mean it, nobody's hurt, I won't do it again,' but some females don't get the tone right. For instance, 'Nobody's hurt,' said soothingly, reminds the Male that all has turned out well, 'thanks to him' is implied, his leadership is reinforced and relationships are restored to their normal surface calm. If however, 'Nobody's hurt' is said resentfully, then it is a challenge to the male's leadership, suggesting that he is wrong to be angry and that he is picking the wrong person to be angry with. Obviously he then needs to put this dominant female firmly in her place. 'Hit her,' according to Stratos. But this is his story and I'm interrupting again.

'Soon after the Master saved my life, but long enough that my throat felt better, I started my Education.'

Chapter 13

'Are you going to take him to classes?' Nina asked. 'And perhaps I could come with you?'

Denis laughed, throwing his head back and showing all his teeth. 'I could teach them more in a class than they could teach me. University of life taught me and that's what I'll teach him. And he's too big for you to handle on your own. Once I've worked on him, he'll be a pussycat for you, just wait and see.'

'Are you sure, Denis… it's just, I think it's getting worse between him and Fredo and I don't know what to do… I thought perhaps an expert might help me.'

'I've told you, you're too soft. They're just being dogs, that's all.' Denis' voice had the start of a growl in it and Nina said no more. 'Come on, boy, time to behave like a grown-up. Lesson one.'

Actually, things had improved dramatically between me and Fredo, ever since the day when he'd given his usual nips at my back ankles and stayed there long enough to find forty-two teeth gnashing in front of his nose. I didn't do ankles. I followed up the warning with the ear pull, jerk and roll. The little runt had no option but to roll and I waited for the proper submission due me. Older, he might be, but the days were long gone when he was bigger and I had learned from my Master and from Fredo himself everything I needed to know to take over. I held his eyes, blazing my fury at him, so sure he'd admit it was all over that I fell for the quick sideways twist, bark and run, that enabled him to stare back at me from a safe distance, barking defiance. Then Denis arrived on the scene. Both Fredo and I greeted our Master appropriately and this time, I was the one who muscled Fredo aside to let *me* pay homage first. There was no nipping or yapping but I could feel the resistance in his body as I shoved him out of the way. So, victory not complete but merely deferred, I told myself, glorying in the ripple of power coming to full malehood in my body.

Apparently, small dogs don't need Education. Although, you could say that Fredo benefited from mine. When I came back from an hour's Education, Denis thought I should be ignored for a while after having had so much attention. 'Too much attention isn't good for a dog.' So I would seek out Fredo. He had enough sense to hide from me but I still couldn't get a submission from the furball and until I did, I would increase the pressure. It made me feel good, restored my sense of my own power, to close my teeth on his flesh. No-one forgets their first bite, nor the first time they're bitten. Was it you, Sirius, who made me stop? Who squealed like a shrew till the wave of rage in my bloodstream was stopped by the infinite, impenetrable wall of brotherhood?'

'Brother, you bit me, I stopped you,' I answered, but I could have done without the reference to a shrew and some acknowledgement of my response. Some puppy matters were best left forgotten, or at least kept private.

'Fredo was not you, brother. I still felt his teeth marks in my legs from my early days in the house. The way he had stolen my bed, prevented me greeting my Master, snapped me into my place as *his* inferior, even when I showed him nothing but politeness. All this was stored in my memory and allowed my teeth the freedom they had always wanted. I needed to Educate Fredo and he did well to run away, to hide in the small corners that suited such a dog-rat. But he could not hide from my voice and I told him what I would do to him when I found him, when there were no Humans to intervene. And still he defied me, even from his hidey-hole, telling me that he was my boss as long as he lived. 'You said it first, Fredo,' I told him.

'See, Nina,' Denis said. 'They're playing together now.'

'It doesn't look like playing to me.'

'Women!' Denis laughed and shook his head. 'Just as well there's a man around.' I was glad he approved of my putting Fredo in his place. Denis understood the compliment, that I was his able lieutenant, following his lead. He was so strong. Just how strong, I was learning from my Education.

I didn't know what to expect but was curious when walk-time changed completely. Denis produced a new collar, metal with spikes inside. 'That will stop you pulling,' he told me. 'Time to be a grown-up.' And instead of the long lead, there was a short chain with a leather handle. Keen for our walk together, I tried to bound off and received as much pain and jerk in my neck as if I'd actually fallen off the window ledge and been held by the lead. 'Heel,' I was told and the pain went if I stayed so close to my Master I could feel the warmth of his leg. Every time I stopped to sniff, or followed a scent so much as a paw's length away from Denis, pain. If I stayed by his side long enough, no pain and, sometimes, 'Good dog.' I had to work so hard to change all my habits and remember how to keep the pain away that I couldn't manage one aroun+era all walk. My tail was as limp as my neck was tense, waiting for the needles to dig in. When I got home the first time, I was exhausted and just went off somewhere quiet to sleep, not even reacting to Fredo's attempts to reclaim territory with some yaps and nips.

As I grew better at remembering how to avoid pain, how to

please my Master on the walk, I kept more of my energy stored inside, had to concentrate less on staying within the tight circle of pain. Denis added new command words, made me sit, stay, lie down. He put me into position with his hands and gave me the command word that went with it. Then he held me there until he gave a release word. Then he told me to do it without him touching me and if I didn't, he hit me. If I got up before he said, he hit me. So I did what I was told and I was so full of energy that I wanted to explode. I needed to be a leader the way Denis was, and I wasn't strong enough to challenge him yet, so I taught Fredo a lesson when we got back home.

Denis added more and more to what I had to do for him. He took off the lead for short spells and made me walk beside him and behave as if the pain was still in place. I strayed a little once and he hit me. He taught me to give a paw and when Nina used the command and I gave her a paw, she was so happy, she kissed both me and Denis. It was a small thing to allow her and I liked being kissed. I was preparing mentally and physically for the two great challenges in my life. Unbelievably, Fredo had still not given me a formal submission and I was becoming obsessed by his defiant little bark. He now had teeth marks under his eye, on his flank and in his skinny tail, but he still shouted his delusions of leadership at me, even while he was running away.

And my Master deserved the full power of my testing. I would know when it was the moment. I was sure he was strong enough to prove his worth to me and to win but I had to show my own quality in the challenge, for us both to feel self-respect and respect for each other. He had to show me he was someone to look up to.

One ordinary day we were on our walk. I was hot, I was irritable. I could feel the inner wolf fretting at the 'do this, do that' nagging at my actions all the time, longing for freedom, or better still, the chance to tell someone else to 'do this, do that.' We'd gone to the park, where Denis commanded me to lie down. I ignored the spot he'd chosen, because it was in full sunshine and I was already panting like a high speed train. Instead, I chose a comfortable shady position, lush grass under a spreading chestnut tree. Denis' eyes narrowed but relaxed as I held my downstay as ordered. I was comfortable, I relaxed as the breeze tickled my nose with jasmine and broom, my ears with children playing in the distance. I shifted onto my side, a more comfortable position than the alert one Denis liked me to stay in. I could feel his irritation mounting but I could also feel the summer's day lulling me with perfumes and sleepy pleasure. 'Stratos, come!' broke into my daydream. I opened one eye and shut it again. 'Oh stuff it.' I thought. 'I'm staying here. Let him prove himself now. I can't lose either way. If he wins, I have a Master worth my respect and if he doesn't, I get to lie here, drifting asleep in the shadows.'

I'd hardly had the thought when my Master was towering above me. I opened both eyes and glared at him as if he were Fredo. 'No,' I barked at him. And then his huge hand descended hard on my rump. I laughed at him. 'Didn't feel a thing,' I told him, 'too used to it and too big now.' Then he welted my face with a sideways swipe of his hand and I automatically snapped in the air. 'That does it,' he shouted . 'We start here and we'll finish this at home.' The spiked collar was back on my neck and even though I didn't move, Denis deliberately jerked it so the points dug into my neck. I'd forgotten the pain, having avoided it for so long and by the third jerk I was on my feet, desperately trying to keep to Denis's angry pace so as to avoid any more torture.

He hauled me into the house and turned on me as soon as we were inside in the basement. He took off my collar and lead. Thank Dog, I thought. He told me to lie down. I obeyed but I kept my eyes fixed on his, defying him. Then he kicked me, a sharp pain in the ribs. I snapped in the air at his boot. 'You asked for it,' he shouted and he hit me with the lead and the chain, on and on, till I screamed and rolled on my back. He had won! I was scared of him. I worshipped him. I wanted to be like him.

'What's going on?' asked Nina, standing white-faced in the doorway with little Boris, held close to her.

'He needed a lesson and I've given him one. You'll find he won't give us any trouble from now on. Look at him.' I lay on my back, wagging my tail, trying not to put pressure on the parts that had been whipped.

'Did you hit him, Daddy?' Boris asked, tearful and huddling close to his mother.

'Yes, son. You have to be cruel to be kind, with a dog, especially with a big dog like this. When you're a man, you'll understand.'

'I don't want to be a man,' Boris whispered. His father didn't hear him but I did. Nina said nothing, just held her son closer, as she turned him to walk away, leaving us in the basement.

From that day on, I obeyed my master's every word, quickly. I gave Nina my paw whenever she asked but there was a lack of warmth in her voice when she said, 'Good dog' so the action seemed mechanical now. Denis told Nina to put me through my paces so he would be happy to go away on business and leave me with her. 'He's a good guard dog so there's no chance of a burglar getting past this one. I don't think a fly with evil intentions would get past him.' Nina smiled weakly. 'But I want you to feel confident that you can control him so these are the commands...' And with Denis giving orders to both of us, Nina and I carried out a very efficient Sit, Stay, Come and of course, Give Me a Paw. I thought about Fredo. I could feel the day of reckoning coming nearer.

'I'll phone when I get there. Take care,' Denis told Nina and kissed her goodbye. He had a big bag with him and he smelled different from when he usually went to work, cleaner, more excited.

Nina took me for a walk, a short one because we had Boris and Cath with us and they grew tired quickly. Nina didn't let me off the lead but she didn't pull on me and I didn't call up the pain in the points. She didn't talk to me and I felt lonely for my Master. He didn't come back at the usual time and eventually I gave up waiting at the window for him. I lay down where I could watch Nina and wait for my Master. I couldn't see Fredo so I didn't think about him. Bedtime was such a fixed routine now that I wasn't even aware of Fredo's existence unless he chose to point it out to me, which he wasn't stupid enough to do. Morning came, no Master. Walk with Nina and the children as far as the school, which was stimulating for my ears, but I was too well-Educated to move one white hair away from my Nina's side. She wasn't my Master but she held my lead and my Master had put her in charge.

I was left in the garden to amuse myself. I chased some noises outside on the street and barked them away. Through the gate, I attacked the woman in the yellow van, who drove up every day, invading my territory with her hand in a box too high for me to reach - more's the pity. I always won and she drove off as fast as if a giant patou were still at her heels. Then I saw Fredo, lying openly in the garden - MY garden - chewing a root. I sniffed; manure, beetle, celery… it was an interesting root and I was having it. I raced up to Fredo, who was so absorbed in chewing his root that he didn't notice me coming and I barked, 'Give it to me.' He had nowhere to hide and he stood to his full height, about my knee, looked me right in the eye and barked, 'NO!'

It was exactly as it had been with me and Denis, so I followed his example. I leaped into action with some well-judged bites and then demanded submission from the pint-sized irritation. Nina had run into the garden shouting and flicking a teatowel that marginally distracted us, enough that I snapped at the teatowel and unfortunately pierced not only the household linen but Nina's hand holding it. She screamed and held her hand up to suck the blood already flowing, and she backed away from us, which helped me a lot. I really didn't want to confuse Denis by getting Nina involved in male combat. This was purely between me and him. Fredo's eyes showed fear and pain but were still trying to focus on mine as he barked 'In your dreams, cuddly toy!' So I ripped his throat out.

I walked over to Nina and explained to her that there was no other option but she was shaking and beyond reason. She ran into the house and I could see her using the telephone, so I settled down to rest, at the other end of the garden from Fredo's body. I don't like the smell of death. Fighting tires me and I felt like a sleep but I'd hardly closed my eyes when a van arrived. Of course I barked at all the strangers but I wasn't really in the mood for serious guard duty so, because Nina told me to go, and used the command words, I let them put me in the van and bring me here. I won't be here for long. When Denis gets back home, he'll explain everything to Nina and come and get me.'

Stratos hurled his belief to the stars, 'My Master will come!'

'His master will come!' we howled.

'Denis will come,' Stratos bayed.

'Oh my brother,' I whimpered, 'What have you done?'

Chapter 14

If you immerse yourself totally in now, in the present, it is infinite and I lived in the now of my brother's presence. After Storytime, under the stars, we shared our memories of the past, our hopes for the future. We argued about what makes a good master. 'Weak,' he called Marc; 'vicious', I responded, about Denis. 'He will come and then you will see a good master,' we told each other. 'If you had been there when he caressed me and told me I was beautiful, you'd understand,' we agreed.

'Why have they put me in this cage on my own?' Stratos asked me.

'They are afraid you'll hurt other dogs.'

'But why?' My brother's bewilderment was genuine. I told you he wasn't always the brightest bunny in the cabbage patch.

'Your last room-mate is a corpse,' I reminded him.

The chain-link clattered as he hurled himself against it in frustration. 'Only because he didn't submit. Any dog that behaves as he should would be safe in my pack.' And again the fence hurled its metallic clink as eighty kilogrammes of patou shoulder-charged it in full throat. 'Why,' he roared across the compounds, 'why are they afraid of me? It's not fair!' I felt it more tactful to take the question as rhetorical. Some questions are better left unanswered.

'And you little brother,' he asked, more calmly, 'are you afraid of me?'

I searched deep. What sort of dog was I? I had looked away from Jack's gaze right from the start and I was content with my place. It was a hard task to be leader, a heavy responsibility. I searched deep and in my heart, I found Jack's guard over Éclair as she became madder each day, I found the daily order in our pen of eating and sleeping together, our survival together holding onto our beliefs with the death-grip that Stratos had used on Fredo, a terrier like Jack. I tried to imagine myself in combat with Jack but found no sense to it. Instead, I imagined Stratos charging me, not the pup I had known but this full-grown male, bigger than me - I could tell from his voice as much as guess from his puppyhood promise - charging at me with killing fury. Was I scared of him?

'I am scared of what you could do to me,' I answered honestly.

'As you should be,' the roar came back.

'But I am not scared of you,' I continued, louder.

'Why not?' his voice was low with menace. I swear I could see his eyes glowing with night-vision and wolf-anger.

'You are strong and brave, big brother, and you always play by the rules, I am not afraid of you because I understand the rules. You wouldn't take my throat because there is no need; I offer it to you. I would be in your pack'

'Ah, Sirius.' The voice purred at me, laced with fatigue. 'You always rolled so well, taught me to hold back, made me want to be a leader who spreads peace where he walks. You will be uncle to my puppies. With you, I could share even this hell-hole. We could lie shoulder to shoulder against the world.' I wouldn't go quite so far in my confidence - I preferred to sleep peacefully without wondering if someone else's bad dream would tear a chunk out of my body - but I wasn't going to be tested on my answer, so I replied, 'Shoulder to shoulder!' I like to think my brother slept more peacefully that night for being less alone. Perhaps he dreamed of his pack and puppy-making. No dog can be alone without going crazy. And I don't mean physically. I mean alone in his heart, no pack, no master.

I don't know how many starry nights we talked, my brother and I, so different but connected beneath the fur, for always. However many nights we had, they were not enough. But I understand now, that, with someone you love, there are never enough nights together, nor enough days.

And for someone in excruciating pain, like Éclair, there are always too many days and far too many nights, all long beyond bearing, with sleep a mere flitting relief, desperately sought. Jack was worn down by his vigil and had himself fallen into a deep sleep, from which he didn't wake even when Sourface turned up with food. Not even when Sourface went over towards him and Éclair and reached out towards the whippet, saying quite gently, 'You've not been eating - come and get some food.'

Too late, I saw the danger and barked, 'Don't touch her ear!' The others joined me in warning Sourface, Jack woke and jumped to his feet but he was too late.

Sourface had merely laid her hand softly on the side of Éclair's head and the poor bitch erupted with pain, jerking her head round to sink her teeth hard into the arm that had increased her already unbearable pain.

'No!' barked Jack, standing between Éclair and Sourface, whose face was white and set, her mouth a thin line.

'I should know better,' she said as she backed away. 'Show just a little kindness and that's what you get for it. Well that's it for you, my girl.' She looked around, assessing the seven of us coldly, and nodded. 'The vet's coming tomorrow.'

'What does she mean, Jack?' Prince asked.

Jack sighed. 'At last, she's noticed. The vet will treat Éclair and save her. We'll have our own sweet friend back with us in a few days.'

'She didn't sound kind,' I pointed out.

'Obviously she's not pleased at being bitten but now she's seen why, she'll get the vet to help.'

Looking at Éclair, foaming and muttering to herself, bashing her ear against the fence, scratching deeper into the gash she had made above her shoulder, unable to reach the ear itself, I wondered if a vet could really restore the friend we'd known. Jack said so, I told myself. I hoped Marc would come soon. And even Denis was better than this.

At morning food-time, Sourface was wearing a bandage on her arm. 'You,' she told me, 'you've had a bit of luck. Your Breeder's coming for you. I don't get the idea she's very pleased about it but she's coming to get you anyway.' The Princess, I thought. She got me out. But I felt like I'd swallowed stones that wouldn't pass. How would Marc find me? And why had Elodie herself stopped coming to see me? My head churned as I tried to take in the news. Soum de Gaia Human was coming. Then at least Stratos and I would be together again.

'And as for you,' Sourface threw the words at Éclair, without moving any closer to her. The vet's coming later this morning, so eat or not, as you like.' Then the door to the pen clanged shut and we dropped back into somnolence, stomachs grumbling on short rations but sustained enough to get through another daylight.

When the sun was high, Bigwoman and Sourface both came back, with two leads and two conical shapes with straps. 'Vicious ones first,' Bigwoman instructed. 'You muzzle the bulldog and I'll take the whippet' and while we watched, confused, one conical shape was whisked onto Maisie's face and the other onto Éclair, who jumped and tried to snap at the pressure on her face, her jaw constrained by the muzzle.

Maisie was struggling to breathe, her squashed bulldog nose dribbling behind the muzzle. They were leashed and quickly led out of the pen, Jack racing to the door to gaze after them.

'Maisie doesn't need the vet. Something's wrong,' Jack was growling when a wave of voices broke, like the chorus of storytelling but this time my hackles rose as I heard their cry, one I hope never to hear again as long as I live.

'Dead dogs walking!' the howl of a hundred dogs, yaps, bays, barks and yelps crowded the air and over it, the one voice we had heard so often calling us to begin, the tale. 'No,' howled Jack. 'Maisie, Éclair!' and as in our storytelling, every voice hushed. But this time the silence smelled of death and we couldn't fight it with stories.

Painfully, a breathless, muffled voice wafted back to us. 'I should have bitten more children while I could. Don't pine for me, brothers and sisters,' and though the last words were just a whisper on the breeze, we heard, 'Nearly over now Éclair, no more pain, never. Keep walking.'

Jack was stock-still, the very portrait of a terrier pointing, quivering at the game he wasn't allowed to touch. Then he hurled back his head and led the farewell. A hundred voices picked up the echo, 'Good hunting, little sisters.' And I remembered Snow and Stella.

'What sort of Choosing is this?' I asked Jack, my tail limp between my legs, my ears low with fear.

'The Final Choosing,' he told me, shaking, his face the mirror of my own. 'We all get Chosen in the end.' And then we saw Bigwoman and Sourface walking back in our direction with one lead. No muzzle this time. The pens were silent as the women stopped, looking in each one as they passed.

'It's a pity,' Sourface said. 'He's no trouble at all.'

'We've already discussed it all,' Bigwoman replied, nails in her voice. 'We've got six new dogs to place and we've just got to make room. I know it's hard but there's no place for sentiment and we've made our choice. Even now we've had permission from Denis Larime to put down that monster of his, we will only just have enough room. At least that will give us the single pen back, which is useful. Nice man, Monsieur Larime. He blames himself you know, for leaving his wife with a dog too big for her to handle. Says she's always been too soft with the brute and he should have guessed she couldn't cope.' They were in the pen now. 'Anyway, this one's got to go. He's just too old. You know he'll never find a home. Prince, here boy.' Prince bounded over to Bigwoman and let her put the lead on him, his eyes the same pools of friendship that had first touched me lightly in greeting. The stones filling my guts had blocked my throat and I couldn't speak.

Prince paused before the door and jumped to lick my nose. 'You'll be all right, big boy.' Then he turned to me, Jack, Melba and Clementine and shook his head as if a tree had unloaded a shower of raindrops on him. 'Don't pine for me, either,' he barked, 'My family is waiting for me. Nothing can part us any more. What is to be will be.'

'Come on,' Bigwoman pulled him impatiently, 'walk.' Without another backward look, Prince walked out.

Jack squared his shoulders and once more the terrible chorus started up for Prince as he passed in front of one pen after another until we heard footsteps on the gravel path in front of the centre building, and then we howled our last farewell before we heard the centre door open and click shut.

Then we waited.

'Is it over?' I asked.

'I don't know,' was all Jack could tell me. We waited eternity. Not one dog panted. Not one dog scratched. We would have heard it if he had. But what we heard was the sound of a hundred dogs listening. You Humans don't understand listening but even you can hear it, without realising. If you're concentrating, you know the exact moment when you have lost someone's attention, don't you? That's because the sound of listening has gone. It is a tension in the airwaves, an invisible connection between the listener and what he is listening for or to. Our listening that day was so powerful you could have snapped it with your paw and seen it break. But no dog broke it. What broke it was the sound of the centre door, of footsteps, stopping outside a pen and then there was a cry more terrible than the ones I'd already heard.

'Sirius!' My brother's roar exploded my heart full of rocks into a furnace. I hurled myself against the walls, against the door, willing them to break before my bones did but I couldn't reach him. The sounds of snarling, snapping teeth and shouting told me that Stratos was putting up a fight but his muffled voice told us all we needed to know. 'When Denis comes, tell him I waited for him. Tell him I'm a good dog. Don't let them lie about me!' His voice was frantic even through the muzzle.

'I will tell Denis!' I howled and Jack, with a glance at me, turned it into the chorus, taken up by a hundred voices. 'We will tell Denis,' promised the pack and then 'Dead dog walking!' started up all from all the pens.

The crunch of gravel, my last moment and suddenly I knew what I had always wanted to tell my brother.

'You are someone to look up to, my brother,' I bayed. 'Good hunting!' and with the click of a door my body split in two like a tree-trunk hit by lightning. I toppled to the ground, and knew nothing. I couldn't even tell you whether more dogs walked. I had learned Éclair's lesson.

All I know is that later that day, in the afternoon, visiting time, the Soum de Gaia Human came to our pen with Bigwoman.

'Strange,' said Bigwoman, 'we rarely get Pyreneans and

we've had two at once. Had to put the other one down this morning. Too vicious for adoption according to his master, who's just back from a business trip to find that the brute turned on his mistress while the master was away. Nasty bite apparently. Thought they were supposed to be a gentle breed?'

'They're still dogs!' snapped a familiar voice. 'It depends on how people treat them.'

Bigwoman gave a curious look. 'The owner sounded to me like he was experienced with dogs. But you know the breed... Perhaps you could have saved this other one then?'

Soum de Gaia Human glared. 'It's bad enough taking one disturbed dog from a S.P.A.. God knows what I'll do with him but he's my breeding and I accept the responsibility - and I'll tell you straight, 99% of Breeders wouldn't come anywhere near you. If we're not careful, every owner who can't handle their dog comes running straight back to dump it on the Breeder. So there's no way I want some other Breeder's aggressive failure to add to my own, thank you very much!'

'I take your point, and we are grateful that you've come for Sirius,' Bigwoman oiled her voice over us. I barely lifted my tail as the lead was put on me. Sirius de Soum de Gaia, 'disturbed dog from a S.P.A.', 'aggressive failure'.

Brave little Jack staggered to his feet, rallied Clementine and Melba to wish me a proper farewell but the words stuck in their throats and we just waved tails, needing no more than that. Surprised by the lack of protocol, the two newcomers who must have arrived without me even noticing gave me their polite 'Good hunting, brother' and I forbade myself all thought, fixing instead that last image of Jack and the labradors. 'I will never forget you,' I told them then responded to the pull on my lead.

As we walked past the pens towards the centre, my heart

quickened. A black mongrel gnashed at me from the single pen, where a notice still proclaimed, 'Stratos, Pyrenean Mountain Dog, subject to veterinary follow-up for biting mistress. Waiting master's return before being put up for adoption. Will need experienced owner, preferably dog-trainer. ' Neither woman glanced at the notice as we walked on the gravel path, through the door that clicked shut and out the other side of the centre to the waiting car.

Chapter 15

My Breeder didn't speak to me once during the whole journey and I didn't care. 'Marc will come,' I told myself as I licked my pads, already sore from clawing the pen walls. I chewed at the muddy tufts of hair and spat them out, then curled my tongue deep between the claws and rasped away until I could see raw pink skin and feel pain. So I could still feel something.

Although I would continue to fill out for another year or two, I was almost full size now, and I could see out the car windows while still lying down. To the side, roads, trucks, cars rushed past me, screaming the zoom of traffic amid the whiff of hot asphalt, exhaust fumes, diesel and that vile artificial orange smell emanating from a little ball swinging from the driver's mirror. Why do Humans overlay interesting organic smells of dirt and decay with artificial orange and vanilla? The clash is an offence to the nose - and that's if it survives the first onslaught of spray chemicals, which have the same effect as does nuzzling ice-cubes.

In the distance, a heat haze hung over the mountains, my mountains. Pic de Viscos, Pic de Néouvielle, Pic du Midi de Bigorre, Pic de Macaupera. the Vallée de Rioumajou, the Val du Lavadon... the old names soothed me like a brush over my fur, gently gently teasing out the tangles. I fell asleep.

To be woken by the car stopping and my Breeder's first curt

words. 'Out you get.' I obliged. And here we were, Soum de Gaia Kennels. The farm had shrunk. The yard where patous and a couple of collies were milling; that pen yelping with puppies - had I really spent my first weeks there, with blue rabbit and green rabbit? Even the acacias tree seemed to have shrunk. The chatter of jays in the orchard made my tail flick with amusement as I remembered Septimus and his Choosing but I flinched aside from the other memories that brought.

I skittered as we walked past the pen and excited littl'uns, fearless and yapping, pressed tiny button noses against the fencing. So had we been, my sisters, brothers and I. Oh, my brother. No, I didn't relish going into a pen. We walked on, past the fence around the yard, where the dogs clustered round the gate, peering at me.

'Sirius,' barked a voice in greeting. Young, female.

'Snow,' I responded.

'What are you doing back here?'

Before I could answer, an older female voice spoke, coldly. 'He let down the family name.' Mother. My tail and shoulders drooped.

'You shouldn't believe everything our Human says,' Snow snapped back at her. Now this was new! 'I've heard plenty at the shows and I'll tell you that our great family name has some very dodgy stories buried in the garden.'

'And *you* shouldn't listen to gossip! Humans at shows are just jealous of our success!'

'Oh, never mind all that now. Sirius I am so pleased to see you, little brother, and it's *your* story I want to hear, from your own throat, not some Human version!' She stuck her nose between the bars of the gate and we made contact, briefly, before my Breeder - I could no longer think of her as my, or even our, Human - pulled me on past the gate.

'Walk on, Sirius. I can't risk a strange male with my dogs.' I added 'strange' to my description.

'Where are you going?' barked Snow, running along the other side of the fence, alongside me. 'You stupid Human, bring my brother in here now! I want to talk to him! He hasn't changed one bit and he gets on with all the other dogs!'

'It's no use,' I told her, 'save your barks for bedtime. We'll talk later. I'll still hear you even if I can't smell you or see you.' Storytime, I thought, with my sister.

'I hate her,' Snow barked. 'She doesn't know us at all. All she thinks of is money. She's probably even confusing you with Stratos.' My throat closed on the name. I couldn't talk about him.

'We'll talk later,' I managed as we moved beyond the corner of the fencing, where Snow could follow me no longer.

'Later,' she promised and I was led away from the farm, the pens and up to a shed on a hillside, with a trough beside it and some chickens pecking around the trees.

'Think yourself lucky you're alive,' my Breeder told me, as she attached a chain to my collar and staked it to the ground, within reach of the hut, within reach of the water trough and out of reach of any Humanity. Was I, I wondered, lucky? I lay down and waited for nightfall.

As I expected, I heard my sister's greetings on the evening breeze. But then they became louder and louder until a white shape rocketed into view and straight into a spat of paws and mouths. Panting, my sister disengaged and stood there, outlined in the purple light against the mountains.

'You're beautiful,' I told her.

'So they tell me,' she shook her little mane of white hair, 'every show-time.' She danced around me, jumping sideways to nudge me and then settled to licking my muzzle. I returned the gesture. She smelled exceptionally female and when I got a bit too personal in my contact, she pushed me off and danced around again. 'Cut it out. I can't believe I escaped so easily! I've been wondering if I could ever since I came back from Tarquin's and I just dug under the fence. It felt soooo good, scrabbling up all that dirt and then shimmying through the gap. Freedom. Of course Mother was telling me off while I was digging but she has no control over me now, you know.' Even from the little I had seen of my grown-up sister, I could imagine. 'I can't believe you're here Sirius - it' so good to see you!' And she rolled me again.

When had I last played with another patou? When had I last played with any dog, rolling on the grass, pinned down and snapping air or on top and flattening my willing partner. It had been too long and Snow indulged me in a long wrestling match. My chain hampered us but we made it part of the game, twisting round it to unblock a pinning move or to catch a slow ankle in its loop. Snow even took it in her teeth and dragged me in a circle till I turned on her. She was wild that night and it's a miracle we didn't do each other permanent damage but her scent both excited me and warned me off, told me that she was in charge, and set limits, however extreme, on our grappling.

That's for Éclair, I gnashed my teeth and power-charged my sister. That's for Prince, I leaned my full weight against her until she rolled. That's for... I gripped her ear in *his* favourite hold, tugged her in a circle, lower and lower. What she was fighting in her turn, I have a better idea now, but it made us well-matched that night in our mad release of energy. Whoomp! The breath left my stomach as she threw herself onto me, going for my throat. And I let her. And I loved it. And I didn't care about the additional bruises to my already battered body, or the nick she left under my eye when she misjudged my flashing turn. 'Woops,' she said, then leaped again.

Finally, bodies heaving with exertion, both panting at express speed, we lay side by side watching the sky darken over the mountain and more stars appear. 'They're always there you know, it's just that you can't see them.'

'Same old Sirius,' she snuffled, rolling on her back so the cool air played along the bare speckled skin of her stomach.

'That's what we're made of, stardust, and that's what we go back to…'

She rolled back onto her stomach. 'Don't get all philosophical on me. There's too much I want to tell you and I don't know if I'll be able to come very often. First I'll give you all the news I've got, then it's your turn. Stella is doing her bit in America for the good name of Soum de Gaia.' That cynical note was in her voice again.

'You wouldn't believe the way they powder and primp patous for shows over there, no respect for us as working dogs. And the Americans are such a different shape, they might as well be a different breed. But Stella seems happy enough if you believe what her Master tells our Human.

And I often see Savoie-Fer at shows. He is stunning, wins all the prizes. Mother says he's the image of Father but I don't trust her judgement any more. She's just so … biddable. She believes everything our Human says even when it's obviously a pack of lies.

Anyway, it's been difficult for Savoie-Fer coping with all the rumours but of course he has his own bitches at his kennels, so he doesn't have to mate outside. His first litter is due next week so you're going to be an uncle.' An uncle to his puppies. So many words had claws now and I was so raw.

She cast her expert gaze over me. 'You're not bad-looking yourself, you know.' She rolled lazily again, chewing on a grass blade. 'And what about you? Seen any of the others? Or heard what they're up to?'

Now was the moment. But that final Choosing lay like a gash across my throat and I was afraid of opening it again. 'No,' I replied. My hesitation passed un-noticed.

'I bet they're just having fun with their Masters, lucky them.

Do you think Septimus has learnt to fly?' And then the reminiscences flowed. When you really go way back with someone, you don't have to tell a whole story or even finish a sentence. Just 'Do you remember Stella and the puddle?' And both of you are smelling the same mud and angry, wet puppy, hearing the same squeals, watching the same pictures running again in your mind.

Sometimes one of us would have a detail that the other had missed, or a different point of view. Snow was surprising me more and more.

'I can't believe how you've grown up. You were such a stuck-up little bitch,' I told her frankly, 'always dangling your good luck in staying, like a bone we couldn't have.'

'Yes, I was, wasn't I.' She was totally un-phased, so sure of herself. I wasn't surprised that she won so many titles. She reminded me of *him* in her self-assurance and once more I was tempted to try and tell her but the moment had gone. Why spoil her night, her life?

'But if it's any consolation, staying here wasn't quite the heaven I expected.' No, I decided again, far better to lie here and listen to her account of jealous rivals and threats of poison, ears lying too low and triple dew claws. I let it all wash over me while the stars brightened over black silhouettes of mountains.

'Sirius, can I tell you a secret?'

'Mmm.'

'I've got to go before dawn in case the Human comes looking for me here. She'll definitely look for me. I'm worth too much money for her not to. I'm running away for as long as I can and I'm going to meet someone.'

'A new Master?'

'No, silly, a dog. A clever, tough dog who works on the next farm, herding sheep. He came to see me last week and promised me...' she was rolling again '... never you mind what he promised me but that's why I bit Tarquin.'

'Wow... slow down, girl. That's not how you tell a story.' And I should know. 'Start with who Tarquin is, then go on with biting him.'

'Wish I could.' Snow snapped at a passing midge. 'Tarquin is just one more beautiful patou from one more oh-so-aristocratic line. Oh don't get me wrong, I appreciate a beautiful patou as much as the next girl but I've learned a thing or two on the show circuit and I don't want puppies with some bad-tempered thug, however good his coat is! And as if his temper wasn't enough to put you off, he's a -,' she growled his pedigree name in a low voice.

'So? Isn't that good enough for a Soum de Gaia or what?'

'You really have been in the sticks haven't you! No-one who cares about puppies would touch that bloodline. I've heard the Humans say it's getting worse too; more and more puppies are being born with dislocated knee-joints and everyone knows it's genetic.'

'But I don't understand. Why would your Human want a marriage between you and Tarquin if he's all you say.'

'I told you - money. Our Human doesn't have any other way of getting money than us and puppies are worth more money if they have Champion parents.'

'Like Father.'

'Yes, except Father was healthy and right in the head not like that overgrown overfluffed bad-tempered airhead I was expected to roll with! But Tarquin the Wonderboy is a Champion and my coat is apparently 'capable of improvement' according to Mr Gedes, the Judge at Lyon. Judges! Now that's another story!

And our Human chooses not to believe anything bad of Tarquin's mistress. And of course Mother goes along with everything our Human says. You wouldn't believe how submissive she is!

So there I was, alone with Tarquin the Great and him expecting me to cut the chase short and roll quickly. Some hope! He got his chase all right and I turned round and bit him good and proper when I'd had enough.

His mistress came running then, shrieking that I was a bad-tempered bitch - me! - and not suitable for her little sweetie-pie, who was looking at me with killer eyes!

Little sweetie-pie was led off in a very bad mood and I had to go home with our Human, also in a very bad mood, and muttering about artificial insemination. Well I want healthy happy puppies and I am off to have some fun!'

'This 'someone,' I ventured, 'you said he herded sheep.'

'At least you listened to some bits. Yes, he herds sheep. Don't you start with the 'he's not good enough for you'. I've had enough of that from Mother ever since she saw him doing what she called hanging around in a shady manner.'

Bluntness seemed to be the only way to find out so I bounded straight in, 'But patous don't herd sheep.'

'Never said he was a patou.'

Now I was shocked. That was really going to put the wolf among the Soum de Gaia chickens.

'So what is he?'

'Collie,' she almost purred. 'Black and white, black patch over one eye and freckles on his nose. And so determined. Good jumper too. You wouldn't believe how cute he is.'

'I hope you know what you're doing…'

'No idea. But I think I'm going to enjoy it whatever happens. Your turn now, properly, right from the beginning. I want to know everything that you've got up to.'

And so once more I told the story of my life. Every time you tell your story, it changes because you have changed, because your listeners of the past are in the story too, because the light shifts on the mountains.

Then there are the parts of the story that you can't tell but *you* know they are there, like the shadows of clouds on the mountainside, there even in the blackest night for those who know where to look.

Chapter 16

When the first rays of sunlight brushed the mountains, a warm tongue licked my muzzle. 'Au revoir, little brother.' And she was gone, a flicker of white elegance dancing across a meadow. If I had to choose one image of Snow that would be it; the moment when she paused, one paw lifted and her head high as she scented the path to take. Behind her, the peaks were touched with fire and beneath her the meadow grasses mingled with late summer alpine flowers, tiny dots of purple, blue and yellow. Queen of the mountain, my sister, snow white. Lucky collie. Or perhaps not. I hoped, for his sake, that he could live up to his promises.

As Snow had predicted, my Breeder was puffing up my hillside before the sun was much above the mountains, head furrowed. She brought food for me and I wolfed it. Was it just yesterday I thought I could never eat again? How the body betrays the heart and carries on, against your will. My Breeder's thoughts were elsewhere and she looked carefully round my shed and territory. Carefully for a Human, that is, unable to see or smell what she was searching for. Two patou-shaped patches of earth lacked morning dew and still felt warm to the touch. Claw-scrapes in the ground indicated the wrestling matches of two patous, with different-sized paws. And how could even a Human not notice the intoxicating smell, like fire-works in your brain, unmistakably Snow at her wildest.

'I suppose that would have been too easy,' muttered my Breeder. She came over and I wagged my tail feebly, automatically. She patted my head and my tail lifted, hopefully. Efficiently, she checked my ears, my body, my paws, either not noticing last night's scratches or putting them down to events in the S.P.A.. 'Could be worse. You won't be seeing other dogs out here so we'll forget the boosters, save some money there, but I suppose de-wormers wouldn't hurt, once or twice, and I'd better keep your coat reasonable... I can probably manage that. I can ask around but no-one's going to be begging me for a full-grown male with behaviour problems... and the puppies come first. Better phone around, see about finding that little bitch. All you do for them and what do you get back?' My tail drooped of its own accord. My Breeder checked the water in the trough and left.

It was no hardship to drowse in the shade, shifting position as the sun and shadows moved, idly opening one eye to see patterns in the clouds, or, eyes closed, listening to the worms tunneling beneath me in their busy work. I lay on the earth where Snow had been, hoarding the warmth, breathing her smell, staving off the loneliness. My Breeder had left a bucket full of food so I topped up when I felt like it, then lay down again, letting my bruised body start healing. From the distant barks of the dogs on the farm, I gathered that Snow was still missing. None of the barking was for me, not even Mother. Or perhaps, if I was to believe Snow, especially not Mother.

As the sun dropped lower, I felt restless with twilight. I tested my boundaries - four dog lengths in any direction, into the hut if I wanted, or as far as the shelter of two small fir trees outside. I could run a maximum of ten steps before a jerk on the chain stopped me. What had seemed merely part of the game last night now chafed at my spirit more even than at my body, and already I'd fretted my neck sore, rebelling against the chain. I remembered Stratos and his collar with points and how he'd accepted it. I thought of Jack, turning his bitterness to leadership, to responsibility for his pack. I searched for their strength in myself and found the calm to walk in my designated circle. At least I could sleep in the cool breezes beneath the stars.

When the sun was above the mountains again, my Breeder returned. Her brow was even more furrowed. Good, I thought. She filled the bucket with food. She checked the water. She didn't pat me. She left. What's new, I thought. There are no bars and I can see my mountains but I don't have Jack, Prince, Maisie, Clementine and Melba to keep me sane. I shied away from my last memories of Éclair. It's all the same. Another Sourface comes and feeds me. I make myself exercise in my too-small territory and I go slowly crazy. I know I must not go in the same direction all the time, that I must vary what I do, but how long can I keep this up and still be Sirius? Till Marc comes?

The routines were already starting, inevitably. Morning saw me in the shade from the hut, afternoon in the shade from the fir trees. I listened to the worms and that gave me my idea. That was the difference between here and the S.P.A., where there had been nothing but concrete. I would observe the tiniest detail of the world around me for there was a story in everything; in the line of ants gathering seeds and trekking back to their nest, each one burdened with twice his weight; in the wooden sheen on the old fir cones, glowing like candles, ready to drop in the next month; in the different cloud shapes, fluffy piles like litters of puppies or long gray strata like silver limousines that flashed past on the motorway. And then I would sing the day at twilight and Storytime, tell it all to the rabbits, the insects and the stars, tell it for the pleasure of the tale, whether anyone was listening or not.

That night when the mountains turned violet and my body surged with youth, I called my strange pack, as Jack had taught me, and I howled the story of my daily universe, shaping my existence with the telling of it. And the mountains gave me the echo, so that I was not alone.

So began another day in exile from the world of men and dogs. You get used to anything in time, Jack had told me, and I was already naming not just my mountains but my two fir trees, the hut, the ants themselves. Then, that twilight came the other change that was to keep me sane for longer than I could have dreamed possible. I started my twilight call and was answered, not just by the mountains but by the voice I already knew so well, however short the time we'd been back together.

'I hear you, my brother. I have a story to tell.' I could tell from distance and direction that Snow was back at the farm but she still sounded buoyant.

'Let us hear the story of Snow,' I announced to the mountains, the trees and the stars.

She was faint but clear. 'Through thickets whose thorns tangled my fur, across brooks whose pebbles slipped beneath my feet and over hillsides which panted in the scorching sun, I tracked my lover, following his signs. If he had come this way for me then I would be as strong, as agile, as wily, for him.

I stopped short at the whinny of horses and cluck of chickens and hid, but my scent alerted the farm dogs, who barked an alarm loud enough to wake a bear in winter. Then I heard rushing through bushes towards me, something faster than I was, and I turned to face the danger. Two collies erupted into my little clearing, one of them my Rockie, a fraction ahead of the other. 'Keep back,' he barked and whisked around between me and the other dog, hackles up.

'Mine,' he growled, 'she's mine.' The other dog opened his nostrils wide, sniffed again. 'Prove it,' he answered, showing his teeth. And then they leaped, clinched in a fury of noise and teeth that moved as one dog, snapping, biting and releasing too fast for even me to judge who was stronger. My head dizzied with their smell and raw masculine power, and I couldn't move. It was as different from being taken to Tarquin as blue rabbit was from a real one and I was suddenly afraid. Was I ready for this? But in coming here at all, I had offered myself and must accept the consequences.

As suddenly as it started, it finished. The loser yelped and turned tail, the winner helping him on his way with a last snap at the departing tail. Then he turned towards me, his eyes blazing from the fight. 'What took you so long?' he asked, stalking me as I backed away, playing for time. Then playing for the sheer fun of the chase. Then I decided it was time for other sport to begin. And so we played the ancient games together and I don't regret it for one minute. It was the right dog at the right time and I don't care one bit what our Human says about sheepdogs.

I don't know how long we had together but we spent nights under the stars and days looking for food and water. Rockie jumped a stable half-door and stole something to eat but we were both getting hungry by the time Rockie' owner saw him and called him home. We both knew the game was up and I followed Rockie into the house, where we were given food and water. 'Say goodbye, boy, you've work to do,' his Master told him, 'and I don't think either of us is going to be popular when this one's owner comes for her. Though I can't say I blame you, you rascal, you.' My lover gave that 'busy, busy' skip and tail-wave that all sheepdogs do, his pointed muzzle open in laughter as he barked at me, 'Till next time! You'll always be welcome, Princess! Stay in touch.' And then with a whisk and another skip, barking with excitement, he was off to work and the door was shut on me. I settled to wait, shattered, and as warm inside as if I'd stolen and eaten ten meat pies from the farm kitchen.

Our Human appeared, with the grimmest face I've ever seen. I thought she was going to hit me, which she's only done once or twice and then it's been less than a flea-bite. She controlled herself though and put on her false face, the one she uses for shows and selling puppies. 'Oh thank you for calling me,' she simpered. 'I've been so worried - she's very precious to me.' You can say that again, I thought, still feeling too warm and full to be annoyed with her.

As soon as we were out of sight, she put her grim face back on. 'To the vet's with you, young lady!' she told me and we went straight to the surgery. The vet and our Human talked about cross-breeds, shows, mixed litters, future problems and it all ended up with an injection and home again.

Where Mother has cold-shouldered me for days, commenting to the air about the 'cheap behaviour of some bitches'. Where our Human has put up ribbons to stop me getting out again. Well, of course, you can imagine what I thought when I saw the ribbon. I headed straight for my hole but it had been filled in. Nothing daunted, I started digging again, brushing against one ribbon very low down. When I touched the ribbon, a storm went right through my body, making me jump with shock and pain. I started digging again but the same thing happened. I can't get past the storm ribbon. Which means I can't come and see you again, little brother.'

I felt the storm ribbon send a shock through me too. But I wouldn't show it. I wouldn't let the Sourfaces of this world win.

'Only Humans need to see each other,' I barked. 'We have Storytime and that's when we will listen out for each other. Sleep well, my sister.'

'Marc will come,' she answered and my own belly filled with the warmth of ten

meat pies stolen from the farmhouse kitchen.

And so the new way of life established itself. My Breeder visited me not every day but regularly, ensuring I had food, water, and was brushed every now and then, efficiently. I could not stop my tail moving hopefully when I saw her, or responding with half-shut eyes to the pleasure of a brush on my fur, but we understood each other. This was a business arrangement. She had done her duty and protected the good name of Soum de Gaia, so that everyone would know she was a responsible Breeder and she would gain twice on her reputation; once from a bad dog like me being safely out of the public eye and once for her generosity in looking after me.

'What rumours?' I asked Snow one evening. 'You said Savoie-Fer had suffered from the rumours. What's wrong with being a Soum de Gaia?'

'He's not suffering now,' she answered, 'not now that he's Vice-Champion of France and Spain. I'll tell you what's wrong with the name of Soum de Gaia - pink noses and white dogs and you know what that means.'

I wasn't that ignorant. 'Lack of pigmentation, genetic link with deafness so lots of deaf dogs. But our Human,' the word 'our' felt like slime on my tongue but that was how Snow knew her, so I carried on, 'knows all that. She said at the Choosing how good our pigmentation is, how important it is not to breed for all white...'

'*Now* she says it, *now* she even does it, but I've heard the talk, especially from the people who have to find homes for them and support their owners. There are too many deaf Soum de Gaia round France for her not to have bred them knowingly.'

'But why would she want to breed deaf dogs?'

'The same reason Tarquin's Human breeds dogs with dislocated knees. Because they're just the rejects, the percentage you dispose of to get the beauty queens, to get *us*, dear brother. And all-white patous were easier to sell, more likely to win the shows, made it worth the rubbish that had to be sneaked out the back way, once it showed signs of handicap.'

'So is it in us, are we carrying all these genetic problems for our puppies?'

'All dogs carries genetic problems for their puppies, Sirius, even the most mixed mongrel you've ever met in the S.P.A.. Just as we all inherit them from our parents. It's the condition of life itself, to accept the inheritance, good and bad. From the moment I thought about motherhood, I accepted that. But if Humans choose for us, they have a responsibility to choose well.'

'She couldn't be so callous... could she? I mean, she loses puppies - and the reputation of Soum de Gaia - and money.'

'The faults don't show up till the puppies are old enough to be with their new owners - that's why she's keen to get rid of them so quickly, won't keep them a day over the eight weeks. And as long as we're champions, there's always new Choosers who'll come to her and be sold a pup. So every time I win a show, I make her more likely to risk my puppies' health.'

'Why don't you throw the shows then? Bite the judge or something?'

'Believe me, I've thought about it, but you were right when you said we're a good litter. Oh Mother's got the bad blood from the old days but meeting Father really was the best thing that could happen to her. It was an outside marriage that seems to have created something special in all of us, beautiful *and* healthy. I've talked to Savoie-Fer about it when we meet at shows and we've been over it again and again, what we should do for the best. And his Human is exceptional. He's rescuing the best of Soum de Gaia by keeping Savoie-Fer as THE male for his own beautiful girls - I just know the puppies will be wonderful. So I'd be hurting him and his pups if I threw the titles…

But I'm not going to let *her* fix me up with a Tarquin. Now she's seen what I can do, she might think twice who she leaves me alone with. And as long as I keep my ears open at the shows, I know who to avoid. I can give her a hint about who I might accept, and then we'll see. If I don't put ideas into her mind about a suitable dog, she'll go back to the plan of artificial insemination and I can't fight a vet. But she won't rush into that - she knows it's expensive, difficult and less successful than the natural way. She's ruthless but not stupid.'

I hesitated but she hadn't held anything back from me. 'And Rockie? Do you think you might have his puppies?'

Her voice was a million years old. 'No, Sirius, *she* saw to that with the visit to the vet. Mother approves, of course. But I think I already knew that it was just a girlish dream. At least I had that much. Life goes on. And I'm going to save *her* cherished name,' I wondered if she meant her Human or Mother, 'along with Savoie-Fer, I'm going to make a line of puppies that are break-your-heart beautiful and so sturdy you could throw them in the air and they'd run round when they landed. You wait and see.'

So young and so much responsibility.

'You know what I can't forgive her, Sirius? You remember when we were puppies. She fed us, she socialised us, she did everything she was supposed to do, right?'

Mother or Human? 'Right,' I responded cautiously.

'But she didn't love us, did she.'

I reflected. 'No,' I howled to my sister in the night. 'They didn't love us.'

Chapter 17

E ven you Humans know that real Time is not measured by clocks. You can make it speed up by being busy or slow it down by doing nothing. Enjoyment also speeds up your time just as boredom or pain slow it down. If you go on holiday and do dozens of different enjoyable activities each day, the holiday will whizz by but in your memory afterwards, it will seem to have lasted and lasted because you will have so many different stories to tell yourself about what you did and where you went. The reverse is true if you lie on the beach every day, sit talking each night; the holiday will seem to last and last but in your memory it will be only two moments.

Every puppy knows that the day is long when you are alone waiting for your Master to come home from work, however big a chew toy he left for you. And that you do not think of time passing when you are chasing your Master into the sea, splashing and yelping together. And any dog who has been staked out alone on a hillside has to discover new ways of passing time and new perceptions of time passing. I was no longer a puppy to hang my heart on the appearance of the only Human in my life, not when she mostly ignored me. No, I mostly ignored her in return. And as basic provisions were always there, the appearance of food was equally a non-event. No, I turned my attention to my domain. My body might be chained but my hearing and sight were free to roam.

Nothing was too close or too small for my attention, nothing too distant. I was a patou surveying my domain as patous had done for hundreds of years. Every day brought new encounters. A skinny little viper whipped through the grass on a mission. I held the liquid brown-eyed gaze of a chamois that leaped into my clearing then froze when she saw me. A nod, a flick of a bob tail, then she bounded out of sight again. A rabbit screamed, a fox gave its high sharp bark. Marmots chittered to each other and scampered for cover. A shadow of wings crossed over me and a beige vulture glided overhead, silent carrion-picker. I heard the slow snuffle of a badger tracking through the night and thought of my identity card, which declared me 'blanc/blaireau', white/badger; the identity card that said I belonged to Marc. And there it was at the heart of everything. I wasn't bored, I was waiting. I had company, good company, but I was lonely for my Human, the one who would come.

Leaf-fall was coming to an end and the farm noises were getting closer. My Breeder was extending pens out towards my hillside. I heard the soft whinny of horses and the bray of their companion and soon their whuffle-huffle breath was my company under the trees. I gathered from Snow that the shock-ribbons formed horse-pens and my territory was now in the middle of one such. Then the chickens moved in, roosting in trees and in my shed, when they weren't clucking, pecking or fighting, in a flurry of spurs and stiffened wings. Where the chickens were, there rats followed; and where there were rats, were the farm cats, stalking rodents or tall grass - you never could tell with cats I didn't speak any of their languages but, from observation, I began to understand the breathy friendship of the horses, the busy egg-laying cluck of hens, the purr and rough tongue of a tabby cat. I would lie quietly until a fellow creature lay beside me for the warmth, and then we would just be, no more than that, just two beings in the now of the great universe. These were good moments and something better was coming.

The tabby cat had been acting strangely, gathering leaves, tree bark and feathers, and secreting herself somewhere in amongst the trees. When I heard multiple mewing, I understood. A very thin tabbycat rubbed against me, wowled and rushed off for a short spell hunting. I guessed the wowl meant 'Look after them for me,' as if I wouldn't have! No wolves would come near my growing flock of cats, kittens, chickens and horses. Perhaps two hundred years of Soum de Gaia blood did count for something after all.

From then on, every time Tabby Cat left her litter, rubbing against me as she stretched her limbs before the hunt, I was extra-vigilant. A warning bark or two, just to let them know I was there, was enough to keep most predators away. But some were sneakier than others. I'd already had one twilight run-in with a fox who thought he'd help himself to the chickens and hadn't been put off by my warnings. No, the cool character approached my territory in swift circles, giving his high bark from ten different directions. Like a gullible fool, I went to the end of my chain in each direction, barking what I'd do to him if he came close enough. And from that, he took bearings and worked out exactly what my limits were. Then he slunk in, well short of my chain length, sending a scurry of squawks and feathers as the chickens fought each other to reach their roosts in the trees. Barking mad and helpless, I watched the lunge of his maw and a brown hen grabbed, still complaining from the fox's mouth as she disappeared with him into the dark.

I learned from that not to give away the fact that I was chained but to stay in one position and bark, keep them guessing. Wolves and bears were unlikely to come down from the high mountains but if they did, I was ready. I practised the moves, running the length of my chain and rearing on my hind legs to clash against my imaginary opponent, while the chickens scattered around me in panic. I let my collar grow imaginary spikes - on the outside - and my chain be just one more weapon in my armoury, something I could wear with pride. 'I am the guardian,' I roared, shaking out the full mane of white hair which had grown since spring moult. The reply was in whinnies, yowls, mews, clucks and quacks - yes, ducks had joined the flock, churning a recent rain-pool to mud with their webbed feet.

Twilight, the violet hour, Storytime, was also in-between the day creatures and the night creatures, when one could eat the other, and I had to stay vigilant. Sometimes I had to break off talking to Snow to send a warning out into the shadows and my senses grew ever sharper for danger, always on watch. So it happened that just when Snow was telling me about building plans and show cheats, my sixth sense was aware of swooping wings and, faster than a scream for help, one of the kittens had panicked and was running into the open, mewling as the rush of owl wings descended closer and the great talons dropped into clutch position. Tabby Cat's cry told me she was on her way back, but not near enough, and I roared a great, 'No!' at the owl as I charged towards the two shapes, gnashing my teeth at the white face fixed on its prey. The kitten was trembling at my feet as, faced with seventy kilogrammes of angry patou, the owl suddenly braked and achieved as near vertical take-off as I'd ever seen. Septimus would have been in his element studying the owl but all I thought of was the little one. I picked her up in my mouth by the loose scruff of her neck and padded back near the shed, where I lay her down between my paws.

This was how Tabby Cat found us, me licking her little daughter, who was already shaking off her fear, patting my paws with her little claws. Maternal instinct is always strongest when combined with the fear of loss, and the smell of anguish and relief rose pungent from the mother cat who dived between my great paws, hauling out her offspring, purring, then thwacking her roughly for being so stupid. I merited some hissing and spitting, whether for allowing the owl anywhere near, or for presuming to touch her kitten, or just because I was there and it felt good to hiss and spit, I don't know. But I was also entitled to a double dose of rubbing and purring, which was duly delivered before Tabby Cat berated her daughter all the way back to their den beneath the trees.

From that day on Little Tab visited me, tangling her tiny claws in my fur, rasping her rough tongue on any knots she found. She was the spitting image of her mother, who looked indulgently on as the light of her life whacked a patou on the nose and then skittered sideways. There were five kittens, all bouncing out of their den these days. When Little Tab ran over to me, the others formed a cautious wide-eyed band behind her, scattering like chickens if I stood up or said, 'Boo!' only to re-group and take teeny steps in my direction once more. It is a privilege to watch little ones grow, to re-discover the world through their curiosity and surprise, to feel the life running through their tiny bodies as they pluck up courage, tap you and run away, only to come back, bolder each time. And if one of those little ones grows up to be your good friend, this is one of the treasures life brings your way. I didn't know what to do with the first dead mouse that Little Tab brought me but I licked her as pack anyway. And although she ranged further and further away, so her adventures were beyond my ken, when she came back there was always a warm place for her against my side or, as she'd first discovered, between my paws.

Warmth, or rather the lack of it, was becoming more and more important for the other animals, who didn't have my long, weather-proof coat. First snow was of course sighted on the peaks while we were still in leaf-fall but our nights too grew chill, fresh and starry, with frost sparkling around us at dawn. The shed became popular and the chickens less so; the floor below their roosts in the shed was thick in droppings that smelled of concentrated acid, that oozed black onto your paws if you accidentally stood on it and that made half the shed a no-go area. The cats moved back down to the farmhouse and its fire. My Breeder tied blankets on the horses' backs.

And one night the magic happened.

'Snow!' I barked at Storytime.

'Snow!' she agreed, playtime in her voice. She spared me the details of mock combat in the drifts, of rolling a patou in the deep white covering and we shared instead the pleasures I could know too, the solitary pleasure of spinning to catch the flakes on your tongue, seeing your own pawprints, rolling in a tingle of cold. The snow made us pups again and I longed for a playmate but my sister had never been able to repeat her bid for freedom; however hard she tried, she could not find a way past the shock-ribbon.

The rapture of first snowfall diminished to familiar pleasures as the snow stayed ... and stayed. Winter had arrived and if I enjoyed the cold, I missed the friends who had moved back to the farmhouse, especially Little Tab. Once again, I adjusted to the new now of my life, watching the forest creatures who lost their shyness in hunger, scrabbling through the snow for worms and grubs, or tracking spoor across the white desert. Eyes glowed in the dark, measuring my strength and wisely deciding that my food was not for the taking. Berries grew scarce, vanishing overnight as a swoop of birds discovered them and moved on. No-one could hide in the white, nor hare nor fox, but no-one could move fast on the ground either. The advantage was to those in the air and the great raptors swept the skies, unhindered. The aim was the same but the rules had changed and everyone was adjusting, taught by cold and hunger.

I felt neither, so I lay in the snow and watched my mountains flaunt their winter clothes, shrouded and sombre when the snow was falling then dazzling blue-white sky-snow reflections in the following daytime. Or red-white at dawn and dusk, flooding the landscape with blood. You could shrivel and cower in the shadow of such peaks or you could stand tall, throw back your head and be part of it, know your age-old right to be here, feel the mountains coursing through your veins.

Winter cocooned me in its endless white now so that the melt took me unawares. A tiny white flower drooped its fragile head in the melting snow, alive and pushing upwards, the first round in the annual fight of spring against winter. Little Tab and the other cats re-appeared. She would always be Little Tab to me but of course she was as big as her mother now, and her purring vibrated right through my own body, though she still played the kitten between my paws.

It was during one of winter's late retaliations that Snow gave me the news of Mother's death. She was in her eighth year, not old, but we big dogs do die young. The vet said that her womb had turned septic and she could only have been saved if her Human had taken her to him as soon as the symptoms began, and then she would have needed an emergency operation that may or may not have worked.

So the warm place which had nurtured us before birth and ushered us into this world had turned poisonous. Snow and I sang a proper farewell, told the Soum de Gaia stories, admitted one more to our store of ancestors, but what you don't feel, you don't feel. She had never forgiven me and I didn't know her. Snow seemed to have finally come into her own, and her voice filled with the authority of leader, the Alpha of Soum de Gaia. You Humans think it is always a male who leads a pack. Not so. There are many examples of great female leadership, calm, decisive, fair-minded and I knew better than most that if it came to a physical challenge, Snow could flash her little teeth in a way that would have shocked her show judges. Beauty Queen and leader, she had it all. And with that knowledge came a great sense of being at ease in her own fur. So it was only a question of time before the next news reached me.

First, there was the non-event of my second birthday, Snow yowling to me at twilight that we should do something special. 'There's not a lot you can do on a chain,' I told her.

'Then destroy something,' she replied, typical Snow.

So I did. I pounded a corner of the shed that had been snow-damaged (appropriate, I thought) and when I had bashed a hole through I took some rotting planks in my teeth and chewed on them, savouring the mould and softness of the decaying wood.

'This must have rotted right through! But I can't understand how it happened so quickly!' my Breeder would comment the next day. 'Any other dog and I'd think you had something to do with it, but you're not the destructive kind...'

So I was two years old. As was Snow. Only two.

'I was far too young to be taken to Tarquin,' Snow reflected. 'But of course I didn't think I was. Just another example of *her* greed.'

'So you were too young for Rockie too,' I teased.

'That's different,' she said, as I knew she would, then with a hint of the little bitch she used to be, 'you wouldn't understand.' There was a silence, then 'Marc will come,' she told me.

'Someone will come,' I bayed in return. My faith had shrunk from a glowing core to a small hard nut, un-crackable, but giving me nothing.

The new season of show gossip started again and I noticed

that one particular male was getting rave reviews, and not just from the judges. It was, as I say, just a question of time. Snow was absent more and more from Storytime and dreamily distracted when she did make contact. Her most frequent contribution was 'Sorry, what did you say? I missed that.'

So it came as no surprise to smell her excitement on the wind, hear her weary voice announcing, 'I did it, Sirius, ten puppies! You're an uncle!'

I watched the stars long into that night and my chain chafed me in a way it hadn't done for ages. I thought of kittens growing up and of Snow's puppies that I would never see. But I was a dog not a Human, I had my ears and my nose, and as soon as they could yap, Snow made her pups tell stories to Uncle Sirius, tales of inter-sibling rivalries and friendships, of the pointlessness of blue and green rabbits.

'Some things don't change,' their mother told me. 'And you'll never guess, Sirius. Two of my boys are dead ringers for Stratos and you.'

Perhaps it was sisterly imagination or perhaps it was true. Perhaps two of the family faces had swum the gene pool to appear again in this new generation. I wished them both luck

Chapter 18

This was only the first litter of Snow's puppies that would join in Storytime before their Choosing came. Snow was as fiercely proud in motherhood as in everything else and no pup of hers was allowed to step out of line. She passed on all the old family stories, all the pride in being a Soum de Gaia, but she passed on something more important, too. However much she chivvied her babies, she couldn't disguise the tide of affection that swept over her just at the sweet clean warm-straw smell of little ones, the pat of a tiny paw or the innocent faces asleep in a puppy-pile. After their Choosing, Snow would race round her terrain, hurling last instructions out into empty air and she would fill Storytime with memories of the foibles and adventures of each of her little treasures.

'There you are,' I told her, when she passed on news of such and such a puppy, whose family had sent a photo or some gossip to our Breeder. 'If they didn't go out into the world, they wouldn't have their own adventures, and you wouldn't have all these stories to tell me.'

Snow had stories of her own too, of travel, the show circuit and all the people she met. It was a great moment for Soum de Gaia when Savoie-Fer, now Champion of France and Spain, was eligible for Crufts, and went there. He'd have been proud of the celebrations in the Pyrenees when we heard the news that he'd won not just Best Male but Best in Breed. Snow had explained all the terms to me but I still didn't really understand any of it. I just trusted her judgement and if she said 'We must celebrate' then celebrate we would. If my Breeder found that another piece of shed had mysteriously self-destructed, then so be it.

'Of course he didn't win Best in Show,' Snow explained to me. 'Patous never do. Even the most prettied-up, powdered patou is in a different league from most show dogs.'

'A league of our own.'

'Exactly. How can you compare a patou with a Pomeranian!'

'Perhaps one day…'

'Not in our life-time, Sirius, not till they recruit judges differently. Even with specialist judges, it's almost the same with Best in Breed - male, male, male. Males are bigger so males are better, more patou than us females. No, they don't judge what's in front of them, they look for what they've already got in their heads. Prejudice rules. And I can tell you that they only have to see certain names - yes, including Soum de Gaia - and they're already thinking, 'Hmmm, I can't go wrong if I choose that one,' unless of course the breeder has argued with them and annoyed them - and then they go the other way! And there's more than one judge likes a pretty face and a smile - on the handler, not the dog! Don't get me started. If it wasn't for my puppies and their futures, I'd say to hell with shows, but there it is.'

Snow wasn't the only one discovering motherhood. Little Tab had disappeared in late spring and when I heard the mewing, I knew it was only a question of time before a little stripey band of thieves and burglars played 'Stalk the dog' under their mother's supervision. Little Tab herself always reclaimed pride of place against my body and, with her as role model, these kittens were the boldest I'd ever known, swinging experimentally from my tail if I stood up or batting a fly off my nose with a 'Woops' when they clawed my nose instead.

And time passed. Three litters of Snow's puppies joined Storytime and left the farmhouse. Snow's joy echoed across the mountains when one little girl was Chosen by her Human to stay and Ulla added her little voice to the twilight. Four litters of Little Tab's kittens discovered places on a dog's body that kittens really shouldn't dig their claws into. 'Happy third birthday, little brother,' rang into the night, and 'Happy fourth birthday.' I had forgotten I wore a chain, I had forgotten that I once had a family but there was always the hard nut in my stomach reminding me that I was waiting for something, that I was observing others' lives, not living my own. But I think I'd realised that this might be it. That you could spend your whole life waiting and you just had to make the best of it. My youth was over.

So it was a shock when, having already seen my Breeder that morning for top-up on food, I heard two voices coming up my hillside.

'I've looked after him for nearly three years now - and I can tell you that no other breeder would do that for a dog. You do it for one and every irresponsible owner thinks he can just return a dog when he's had enough, like taking clothes back to the shop.' Same old story. I lay down again. 'Well I can't keep him any longer. This is a working farm and we need the land.'

'Have you tried to find a home for him?' Female, warm, melodic voice, hiding thoughts.

'Well of course, we tried' Big sigh. 'But people want puppies. And I have to be honest so if someone asked about him, I'd have to say that he bit a child. That's why he was in the S.P.A. you know. And as soon as they contacted me, I went running to rescue him. But I have my own dogs to think of and...'

'So tell me about him.' A hint of coldness.

'He's a beautiful dog, a Soum de Gaia of course - I assume you're familiar with our pedigree? His first owners separated and the second owners were probably too soft with him. You need a fist of iron in a velvet glove with Pyreneans, you know. You have to be firm.'

'So I keep being told.'

'I'd forgotten, you know the breed of course. Do you have any yourself?'

'One three-year old I adopted, and a black patou puppy.'

Tinkling laughter. 'Oh, I'm sorry, but that must be a Newfoundland. There's no such thing as a black patou.'

'She *is* a one-off. Dad has never been identified but all she seems to have got from him is the colour - she's pure patou. *Black* patou.'

Audible sniff. 'Well Sirius is a good guardian, marvellous with other animals - he lives with horses, cats, even chickens.' My heart sank. I could see the new S.P.A. notice already, *'Sirius, Pyrenean Mountain Dog, 4 years old. Good with animals.'* Was I really four years old? 'He's not suitable for a household with children, of course.' Of course. 'And I think you'll find that he's quite sociable, although he hasn't seen anyone other than me for some time...'

'For how long exactly?'

'Well... let me see... for nearly three years actually.'

There was a long, cold silence.

'And how is he with other dogs?'

'Obviously I haven't been able to keep him with my dogs...'

'Obviously.'

'... but in principle there's no problem.'

And the two figures came into view and I couldn't help myself. Even if she was from a S.P.A., even if it meant madness in a pen, she smelled of happy dogs and my tail wagged of itself when I saw her and as soon as she came within reach, she held out her arms and said 'You sweetheart, you,' I didn't have to be asked twice. I jumped at her, put my paws on her shoulders, licked her face and she didn't seem in the least bit taken aback. She laughed and scratched behind my ears, blew at me with a horse-noise and laughed again when I shook my head, stood down and wuffed. I went into a play-bowing position and she stamped her feet. I bounced, she stamped her feet again. She ran backwards, I ran towards her - and the chain stopped me. I stood looking at her, unable to get closer and her mouth turned into a narrow slit as her eyes focused on the chain.

Nervous giggle from my Breeder. 'It wouldn't do if he escaped. I told you I take my responsibilities seriously. And he can reach the shed for shelter, he has food and drink, and it's natural for a patou to guard his flock on the hillside. I think that's how he sees all the other animals.' Little Tab chose that moment to pay me a visit and I automatically bent my head down to receive a rub and a purr, and lick her in return before she went off on serious cat business.

'Well aren't you just gorgeous,' the woman said to me, with no trace of the coldness that seemed to come and go in her tone.

'So you'll put him on the rescue website?' my Breeder asked, selling voice back.

'Of course! No question about that.'

'I realise he's too old and there's no hope but at least he'll have had his chance. And I can't keep him indefinitely...'

'I understand exactly what you're saying.' Real frost in the voice. 'I don't think you should be so pessimistic. There's lots of good reasons why a dog might bite a child and of course I agree it's too big a risk for him to go to a family with children, but there's plenty of other homes. And there are advantages to having an older dog. He's house-trained for starters.'

Doubt crept in. 'Isn't he?'

'Well, he was,' my owner answered, carefully, 'but he hasn't been near a house in… some time.'

'I see. Well he's over the puppy stages anyway.'

'Oh yes, and he's not at all destructive, at least not up here…' she tailed off.

I was being treated to some regular back rubbing and then - oh bliss! - the side of my face was being stroked, delicately, from muzzle to ear along the lie of my hair, just the way that I liked it. 'I'd take him myself if I could…but I mustn't, not at the moment, not with a pup to bring up… can I take a photo?'

'Go ahead.'

'It always helps to have a photo. That and a name.' And a really really sad story I thought. Yes, I knew the routine. And I looked straight at the camera. Read this really really sad story, I told the machine, as it clicked and whirred.

Then I had the chance of one last cuddle and I made the most of it, my aroundera saying everything that my eyes hadn't already. 'I'll find someone for you, Sirius, I promise.' I licked her face but that didn't stop me thinking, just one more human promise to add to the collection.

Then they were heading back down the hillside.

'And vaccinations?' the woman asked.

'He doesn't need them where he is now…'

'So you're saying they're not up to date?'

'You could say that… you don't know how hard it is to be a breeder. Last week someone tried to get a puppy out of me for free, told me their own, one of my last litter, had died of parvo-virus, but when I checked with the vet, they'd taken him to be put down because he had a bit of a limp - like patous often get when they're going through the main growth stage - the vet refused euthanasia and found a home for him and of course I sent the couple off with a flea in their ear, but you can't trust anyone these days and they're all about money, money, money…'

I surveyed my animals, my mountains and my stomach churned. I'd forgotten what it was like, the connection with a Human, and now the memory was re-awoken, it hurt all over again. I couldn't stay here, my Breeder had said. I would have to say goodbye to the mountains, to Little Tab, to Snow and Ulla. And I had to face the truth; no-one would come for me. Or worse than no-one. I was heading back to a S.P.A.. I was four years old and I knew what the S.P.A. thought of dogs over five. So that was my future.

When you Humans know you're going to lose something, you react one of two ways. Either it becomes doubly precious or you give up on it completely and can't enjoy it any more because you're going to lose it. Dogs always choose the former. If you see the biggest dog in the world, swaggering towards you, growling, with his eyes on *your* bone, those last teeth-grinding chomps on your treasure are the most satisfying moments you have ever spent with that bone.

Every purr and head-rub, every cloud shadow on a mountain, every story at twilight was stored as treasure in my memory. Even when the wind blew up from stillness, under a blackening sky that rolled over from the invisible mountain-tops and the summer storm cracked open the sky with searing zag-zags of light to a background roar that shook not just my shed but the very hillside itself, even then I was not afraid. Instead I thundered back, rearing up with eyes shut in the rain that fell like stones, pounding on my muzzle. I became part of the storm itself, part of my landscape, the Great Pyrenees. How could I be hurt by weird light that flashed the landscape illuminated and then blacked out as if a great bulb were being switched on and off in the skies? What was there left to be afraid of? What could be worse than what was to come anyway?

I thought back over my life. I remembered how I used to sit on Marc's lap in his low deckchair in the garden, my legs touching the ground as I grew bigger. Then the day Marc clambered into a new seat, slung between two trees. I jumped onto his lap as usual and this seat tipped us both out so Marc was flipped like a pancake to land flat on his face on the floor. Or the day Marc and the vet chased me round the surgery because I didn't want her looking in my ears. Or the night Marc had taken me out for a pee and the door had slammed shut, locking us out. He hadn't dared wake up Christine so we'd spent the night under the hedge, beneath the stars - until the sky clouded and the drizzle started. We'd been drenched when we sneaked in the next morning after Christine unlocked. Marc had rushed to the bedroom unseen so he could throw on some clothes and pretend we'd been for an early morning walk. I remembered the little daily pleasures. When Marc or Christine called, 'Aperitifs!' I would run to the kitchen and find them standing by a huge cold cupboard. They would push a button, then after a whirr and a clink, ice cubes would arrive in their hands and, one at a time, proceed from there straight into my mouth.

And I remembered Stratos. His betrayal. Humans are fond of an old, old story, about a Prince who goes hunting, leaving his faithful hound to watch over his baby son, who is sleeping peacefully in the cradle. When the Prince comes back, the hound greets him, covered in blood and the baby is nowhere to be seen, so the Prince puts his dog to the sword. Then, when he goes further onto his property, the prince discovers the baby, unharmed, in the cradle, and beside him the corpse of a wolf the other side of the cradle, a wolf killed by the faithful hound. Distraught, the Prince watches his dog die. Why do Humans love this story so? Why don't they understand it better? And why don't they at least realise that if it had been me or Stratos, or any self-respecting patou, the wolf would never have got so close to the baby?

Stratos had put his paw on something that I still hadn't quite got clear in my head. He'd worked out what it was that all dogs want. But of course, being Stratos he didn't know he'd worked it out and it was up to me now, to do the thinking for him, to make that his last gift to me. Remembrance, love's last gift. What was it in all that he'd said which kept rumbling away in my brain like thunder in the distance, the storm never quite breaking?

It was while I was puzzling over such thoughts that I once more heard two voices. So this was it. I almost whimpered but I was determined to show more pride at the end. I listened.

'Of course you've heard of Soum de Gaia. We have many Champions in our line. One of my boys. Savoie-Fer, is current Champion of France, Spain and he won Best of Breed at Crufts. And he's Sirius' brother… so you saw Sirius' details on the Rescue website, you were saying.'

'Yes.' Just one word and my heart somersaulted worse than Marc's hammock. I knew that voice. Someone had come to keep a promise.

Chapter 19

If I'd been enthusiastic with the woman who came before, that was nothing to the show I put on this time. When I ran towards them, my aroundera was flagged up so high, I thought my hind quarters would lift off and when I reached my target, I was bouncing on my hind legs, my tongue greeting every patch of bare skin I could find as I barked, 'What took you so long?' with so much excitement I nearly choked. 'Izzie,' that familiar voice whispered in my ear, 'oh Izzie'.

'Anyone would think he knew you,' my Breeder observed.

'Mmm,' was the noncommittal response, as my front legs were placed gently but firmly on the ground and a hand searched for *the* spot below my chin to stroke and scratch. I couldn't stop whining and turning in circles while my tail wagged so hard I thought it would whirl off. 'Would you take this chain off him, please.' My breeder didn't seem quite so pleased at actually hearing a fist of iron in a velvet glove but she obeyed the veiled command. For the first time in five years I was free. At liberty to run away across a thousand kilometres of mountains. And you already know what I did, don't you. I carried on turning in tight little circles, smaller than the chain had ever imposed. I was already where I most wanted to be. It was my heart that was unfettered.

She had changed, my Princess. She was thinner and she

seemed taller, though I think that was an illusion. There was a calmness about her, as if her energy was more contained, but that just made her glow even more. Just as she had all that time ago, she crouched down and held out her arms to me, holding a chain collar and lead. 'Izzie,' she purred, 'come here my beautiful, sweet, little boy,' and once more her eyes drew me towards her and I held her gaze, unafraid as she put my collar and lead on me.

'You shouldn't let him look you in the eyes, like that. It's a dog's way of challenging you and before you know where you are, he'll be nipping and bullying, perhaps worse.'

'So people say,' Elodie replied, holding my gaze. 'Good boy. Down!' she commanded, and I lay down at her feet. We'd had too much fun with command words on the waste-ground for me to forget - and it was worth it to see my Breeder's face.

'I'm just trying to warn you to be careful... these big dogs need expert handling...' I waited for the inevitable but she hesitated and decided against it, '... and as you know from the Rescue site he has bitten a child so I want to be sure you know what you're doing. As I told Rescuemontagnes, you seem very young to me.'

'I'm twenty two, Madame Berin, I have a Diploma as a Veterinary Assistant. I live in the countryside with my parents, who have two spaniels and five thousand metres square in land. For my birthday present, my godfather has offered to buy me a pedigree dog, with my parents' consent and I wanted a Pyrenean mountain dog.'

My breeder's voice was sugary again. 'No doubt you watched Belle and Sebastien as a child... so many of us fell in love with Belle, in black and white for our generation but for yours it's the cartoon of course...'

'No, it was the real thing I fell in love with, not a cartoon.' And her eyes on mine left me in no doubt who was the real thing.

'But, forgive me asking, if you have money to spend on a dog, I still don't understand why you don't have a puppy. I have an outstanding litter ready for homes in two weeks.' Money, I thought anxiously, hearing selling voice. Those steady hazel eyes reassured me.

'I am putting the money to good use, thank you. I don't see the point of spending all my money on a puppy and having none left to train him properly. Sirius is the dog I have chosen, for personal reasons, and I am using the money to go to the best dog trainer I can find in France, so I can learn alongside Sirius. And I aim to become a dog-trainer myself, so you see, that answers your questions.' Elodie told me, 'End it,' and up I got, bang on cue. 'Now then Madame Berin, we have some papers to sign, then I have a long way to drive so we'll be on our way.'

It felt like a procession, walking down the hillside with Elodie and my Breeder, me wuffing farewell to chickens, horses, cats, especially Little Tab of course, but with no time to feel the leaving. Down the hillside to the gate, behind which my sister was barking herself frantic in circles.

'I know,' she told me, 'I know, it's wonderful, I'm so happy for you.'

'I'm happy too, uncle Sizzie,' yelped a youngster and I paused to admire the new generation of Soum de Gaia.

'She's beautiful,' I told Snow, who felt a sudden need to bury her head in her daughter's perfect coat and start the special fine nibbling that we do to groom ourselves or those we have bonded with.

Ulla wriggled free and Snow looked up. 'One more time I wish you good hunting, little brother.'

'Things have changed, Snow. This time I will miss you and it will be ten stolen cakes from the farmhouse kitchen warming my stomach every time I think of you leading the Soum de Gaia with Ulla beside you.' Snow's eyes flashed laughter, acknowledging the reference to a younger, wilder moment and then we rubbed muzzles before I was whisked on into the farmhouse for the paperwork.

'He is in my name at present,' my Breeder said. This was news to me. It meant that Marc had signed me away. One stroke of a pen gave you a family and another stroke abandoned you. Or worse. I thought of my brother, our argument over who had the better master and I apologised to Stratos. Equals, I told him, equally bad. So when Elodie signed to be my family, I didn't feel the same rush of belonging, the same trust as I had first time round. Now, in her presence, I was sure of her love for me, but I had felt the same before, hadn't I.

Can a dog love more than once? I have thought about this long and hard. After all, a dog's famous for faithfulness and loyalty, for dying alongside his master - although I have to say that I have not come across any examples of this in real life, among the many many true stories that have come my way. No, there is no doubt about the answer; a dog can love more than once BUT. It is the nature of this BUT that you Humans need to think about a bit more because it applies to you as well. It is the same BUT as what was missing on our papers at the S.P.A., it is our past that is the BUT, along with all that it has created in us for good and bad. Second-time-arounders have expectations, fears, habits and reservations.

Elodie sweet-talked me into the car where my Breeder gave her brightest smile, all teeth and wished me 'Good luck, Sirius, with your new family.' There had been times I would have liked to give her *my* brightest smile, all teeth, but I knew better than to risk the consequences for a moment's over-rated satisfaction. She was now my past.

And my present was lying along the comfortable back seat of Elodie's car while she talked to me. I had forgotten the pleasure of being talked to, the range of emotions flavouring a human voice, especially when the topic was me. I half-closed my eyes, lulled by the hum of the engine, the vibrations of the car, the whizz of passing traffic and - thank goodness - no artificial orange/vanilla, just the sweet young smell of Elodie and the perfume essence she wore, sandalwood and jasmine, more adult than her previous scent.

Elodie waved gaily to my Breeder as she drove slowly off. 'What a cow! I am so angry I could scream but if I'd lost my temper there I'd never have got you out! Even at the last minute she could have changed her mind and just gone ahead with putting you down. That would have suited her fine, nice and tidy. She gets all the credit for looking after one of her ex-puppies that inadequate owners have turned vicious - or so she thinks - with none of the risks that you'd damage her reputation if you're out in the world somewhere.

And that chain! It's just like Sara said it was. Your body looked after in a minimal way and your soul in hell. Your sad eyes! Oh Izzie, I promised you I'd come for you and I couldn't help it taking so long, really I couldn't.

First of all, that other cow at the S.P.A. got me banned from helping out, and I wasn't even allowed to visit so I couldn't come and see you at all. I told you I'd find out who your breeder was so I did, and I phoned her and she sounded so nice on the phone, so responsible and she was going to get you straight away so I thought you'd be fine and you'd be all right with her or you'd get a home. I did check up. I got someone else to visit the S.P.A. and see if you were still there and you weren't. The other patou had gone too so he must have found a home - I'm not surprised because he was so beautiful. He must have been pedigree too. Strange for you both to be in at the same time. I even wondered if you were brothers.' She laughed. 'Silly idea. I watch too many films. I know he'd been aggressive but there are people who can re-educate a dog and I'm glad he found someone.

Anyway, my friend even asked, to check up on what had happened to you, and she got told that your breeder had come to get you. So I was pleased for you and sad for me because I had this feeling that you and I were supposed to be together. I know that sounds soppy but it's the truth.

But I'd had enough of the S.P.A. Sometimes I wonder if they want to find homes for dogs at all or just to keep the ones they've got in cages forever. I suppose they get bogged down in how impossible the job is but they could do it so much better... so then I started training and working at a vet's and learning, learning, learning.' She sighed. 'And I kept putting off having a dog of my own. There was always something not right, what with living with my parents and their dogs, and me working so hard.

You get to hear a lot when you work in a vet's, not just medical stuff, and people ask you about boarding kennels, about dogs they've found on the road and about putting dogs to sleep for the most stupid reasons. You wouldn't believe it! We run a message board to try and help people and one day someone came in with a web address. She said that if ever there is a patou in trouble, there's a site that helps them and finds homes for them, wherever in France they might be. I'd been thinking for ages and ages about a dog of my own and I just couldn't forget you, Izzie, so I thought another patou might be the one for me, then with my godfather saying that I could have one as a birthday present, it all seemed to fit together. If I had a Rescue patou instead of a puppy, I could afford the best training in France to help me with whatever problems come with adopting a dog and start me off as a dog trainer.

Then when I looked at all the stories, there you were, *my* Izzie, chained up on a mountainside, lonely - even if you did have other animals. And not even dogs for company. I saw how friendly you were with the dogs in the farmyard, which is just as well because you're going to have two wonderful friends in your new home.

And then I'll have to find this great trainer I've told you we're going to, because the truth is, I have no idea who to choose. I've spent hours online reading what trainers say about themselves and just when I think, yes, this all makes sense, there's something that I know is just not true and I don't see the point in going to someone who knows less than I do.' I pricked up my ears at that. I'd heard someone say that before and it hadn't been a good sign.

'This is where I've got to. It's got to be someone with plenty of experience training all kinds of dogs, including difficult ones. I want someone who does the training herself, who doesn't just squeeze a car horn and tell a load of confused masters what orders to give - that just doesn't work. I want someone who doesn't think you should hit dogs or shout at them.' Now I remembered. It was Stratos' master who didn't see the point in classes. University of Life. Surely Elodie wasn't making Denis' mistakes?

Elodie continued, 'I don't mind at all if most of what she says and does is common practice and common knowledge - it stands to reason that if something's good and has worked for donkeys' years, we're still doing it. But if there's so much as one really stupid piece of advice in what she says, then I'm not going to her. And so far that knocks out everyone.

It's all very well, using all this modern observation of dog behaviour to help us give the right messages but some Behaviourists have no sense! You just wouldn't believe what rubbish I've read! 'Pull a dog's ear if she behaves badly, because that's what another dog would do to dominate'. Great way to get bitten. 'Never go to the same level as the dog by sitting or even worse lying on the floor beside him.' So that knocks out all the fun I've ever had rolling around on the floor with Caboche and Jet. 'Don't give your dog too much praise, it will spoil him.' How stupid! 'Never allow a dog onto your bed because the alpha male and female sleep separately.' I reckon if you've got the right relationship with your dog, you can allow your dog to do whatever suits you - that's the point isn't it? But that's also my question, Izzie, just how do you make sure you have the right relationship with your dog? And I'm still looking for someone to teach me.'

The car slowed and I slewed to one side as Elodie flicked the clicking switch and turned the wheel. 'Well here we are. Your new home.'

Perhaps I should leave the story there, the perfect love, the perfect ending. And I know you will say I was ungrateful when I tell you what happened next. But you see, sometimes love isn't enough.

Chapter 20

In the beginning it *was* perfect. When the car boot was opened, I blinked, paused on the brink of this new life, then jumped into my future. Or more literally into the sniffs and yaps of two excited furballs. When you reach a certain age, every new experience has echoes of another, older one that predisposes you to react one way rather than another. One golden cocker spaniel, one black, interrupting each other all the time, brought back the memories and I waited calmly for a pause in the yapping.

'Tell him about the mouse...'

'But he's only just got here - he'll want water first, before stories.'

'No, no, no - introductions before water.'

'But he knows our little girl already.'

'No, not Elodie.'

'David and Adelphe, yes, yes, yes.'

'No, idiot, *us*!' Their little curly tails had left me in no doubt as to their intentions being friendly and my own tail was waving an aroundera in response. 'Caboche,' the golden one barked, 'and the noisy one's my sister, Jet.'

'Sirius,' I said, simply. Of the Soum de Gaia was no longer important.

While I was greeted by the spaniels, Elodie kissed the older man and woman waiting on the driveway. The man, David, came over to me and held out his hand politely, under my muzzle. He smelled of engine oil and spaniel and I let him caress my face and neck, even stroke the top of my head, which normally I wouldn't permit on first meeting. A male has his standards.

'It's all right, Adelphe, you can give him a stroke.' The woman approached timidly and I flinched when she dived her hand down on top of my head, but gritted my teeth and accepted it. My mistress' people were my people. I sensed the human tensions relax a little.

'He seems friendly enough with our two,' David conceded, 'and with us, but I hope you know what you're doing, Elodie.'

'I hadn't expected him to be so… big.' Adelphe said.

Elodie laughed. 'He's a big softie. You'll see'. Then she let me off the lead to 'go and play'. The spaniels didn't need to be told twice and careered round in competitive races of their own devising, encouraged by the Humans who threw a ball for them to fetch.

I tried to join in. I jumped around the spaniels, careful not to step on them and I started to run too. That's when I discovered the invisible chain. I would start to run, then stop, at exactly the distance the chain would have jerked me back.

'Has he got a problem with his legs, Elodie?' Adelphe asked.

Elodie's eyes met mine. 'Oh Izzie. What has she done to you!'

I started to run again and after several run/stop, run/stop fiascos, I found that if I concentrated really hard I could break through the invisible chain barrier. I still slowed down, my body believing in the chain that my brain said wasn't there but at least I didn't stop dead. I was panting with the effort though.

'It will come, Izzie. It will come.' I watched the spaniels, their ears flying as they chased each other round the garden and I lay down on the grass. I was a good guardian and it was something I could do. Elodie sat down beside me, stroking me, telling me how wonderful I was and I rolled onto my back to give her full authority to caress my stomach as much as she liked, just there, where the bare flesh showed.

The spaniels took this as an invitation to them too, which they accepted with the exuberance they seemed to find for every activity. It was a shock to have two small dogs land on me from different sides but we were soon a rolling, scrabbling, play-snapping pile of fur. Elodie jumped out of the way, laughing.

'He's not hurting them, is he dear?'

'No,' replied Elodie and her father at the same time, while I batted alternate dogs off my rear quarters, which they had decided was the safest target for a little harassment. It wasn't the all-out wrestling I'd known with Snow but it was fun and it was such a long time since I'd had physical contact with another dog. I'd thought everything would just go back to how it used to be and my failure to run had shaken me, made me wonder what else had been taken away from me.

Imagine that you are the guest of a tribe in the deepest, most remote part of the Amazon rainforest. You know nothing of their language, nothing of their culture and you know only one person there, who understands you. I followed Elodie everywhere and when I was beside her, I was calm enough to observe this new world. The inside of a house seemed too hot, cluttered with obstacles that made strange noises and I just didn't know where to go for what. One question was answered when Elodie put down a mat in the cool hall and told me 'Your corner, go to your corner.' Then she took me to the mat and gave me a biscuit. She did this a few times until I got the idea and as long as she was nearby, I didn't mind going onto the mat to please her. But if I couldn't see her, I grew anxious. The walls closed in on me, I couldn't fulfil my duties as a guardian because all the noises indoors were threats. It had just been too long since I had lived in a house.

I breathed again when I was allowed outside. Elodie walked with me round the boundaries of our terrain and let me take up position on a rise, where I could see the entry to the house and bark my warnings. She left me there and I accepted the job she'd given me. I was a good guardian and I barked to tell the family each time there was a car in the lane, I continued barking if the car stopped and when one car opened its boot for a dog to jump out, I barked the full wolf warning - every patou knows that stray dogs are as dangerous as wolves for the flock. Elodie came back to get me.

'You're going to have to come in now Sirius or the neighbours are going to complain.' I resisted her as it was nearly twilight and apart from Storytime, every patou knows that twilight and night are the most dangerous times. I wanted to protect her and her family and I certainly knew more than she did about guarding. But she wouldn't listen to reason and insisted, with collar and lead, that I go back into the house with her, where I paced about and worried, until it reached Human bedtime.

Then Elodie took my mat and told me to follow her. She placed the mat by her bed and told me this was my place. Yes, I remembered sleeping beside my Human at night and it seemed right to me. Everything I did had echoes. But I felt too hot, I could hear faint night noises and missed the cool air and the stars. I paced and worried.

'It will come,' Elodie promised me and sleepily stroked my head when I did lie down beside her, too tired to do anything other than sleep uncomfortably until morning.

We went on walks together, hunting further and further afield, in tune with each other. This time, my memories chimed perfectly with the present. My best memories of walks with a Human were of those when Elodie had been beside me. This time she was my signed mistress, the one whose days

I accompanied, whose sleep I guarded. My aroundera touched the clouds, I pranced when I walked, I wanted everyone to see us together. It was all I could do not to whine non-stop with excitement. I'd have played recall, sit, down and stay with her all day long, to hear the pleasure in her voice when I obeyed her. And instead of the wasteground, we had open fields and woods, endless smells to explore. Even a river.

When she took me to the river, I hesitated, looked at Elodie. There was no Newfoundland to lead me or tell me what to do. 'Go ahead little boy. Have fun,' she encouraged me and I didn't need to be told twice. I plunged into the water, enjoyed the shock as the cold hit me, the different currents curling around me at different temperatures and I showed off every trick I knew, with Elodie whooping and laughing on the bank as she watched me. Then, for the sheer pleasure of the exercise, I just powered along with the current, swimming, swimming, swimming… with Elodie jogging along the bank in parallel. That's when I realised something was missing, but this time it was something I was overjoyed to be rid of. There was no invisible chain in the water, nothing that checked me and slowed me down, nothing but the water itself. In the river I was the same young dog I'd once been. And if I could be like that in the river, then I could be like that again out of it, too.

'Look at me,' I barked. 'I'm free.'

'Oh Izzie. It's good to see you having fun! We need to have more fun together.' And the next time we went to the river, Elodie stripped off her outer clothes to a swimming costume and she came in with me. This was a whole new set of games and she didn't seem to appreciate some of the ways I used to play with the Newfie. Lack of fur is a real disadvantage for you Humans. On the other paw, she could swim faster than I could and she could turn quickly too, so she seemed to like the games of chase. Recall in the water was a very different proposition and she seemed more worried than delighted when I responded to it.

'Gently Izzie, gently. You weigh seventy kilogrammes and I'm just fifty! No....' and she lost her footing as I shouldered her. She ducked under the water to come up again spluttering. She could stand up and I couldn't, which gave her a very unfair advantage.

What seemed to please Elodie the most was a game we discovered by accident. She'd rolled onto her back and was floating, not moving her limbs, and it reminded me of all the pretend rescues I'd done with Newfie so instinctively I swam alongside, took her wrist in my mouth and towed her. She was so surprised she struggled and gulped water but then she went on her back again to see what would happen and of course I towed her again. Moments like that kept me going, feeling the trust between us, but it wasn't easy.

Then Elodie told me the holidays were over and she was going back to work. I watched through the window as her car left the drive, without me, and it was as if someone had sliced out part of my brain so that I only had two feelings; panic and the need to get back the missing part of me. I went round and round the rooms of the house open to me, as if it was the S.P.A. cage or the circle allowed by my chain, forgetting all I had ever learned about pacing and the dangers of going mad. The spaniels tried wuffing friendly advice along the lines of 'She'll be back, don't worry' but they had their masters there, they were indoor dogs and they weren't me. David and Adelphe tried to stroke me and reassure me, which of course convinced me that I had lost Elodie forever. I had plenty of supporting evidence for reasoning that way, in so far as I was reasoning at all by this stage. So there I was, seventy kilogrammes of panic-stricken, whimpering lonely patou. And I committed a crime against Humans.

When I did it, Adelphe shrieked so much I felt even more scared, if that was possible and David shouted so much I thought he was going to hit me. Instead, he told me to go outside, I was a bad dog, and I went up to my place where I could guard them to make up for everything and to wonder why I'd done it in the first place, but I knew that, really. I'd been scared out of my mind and everything had smelled wrong, this house I didn't really know with its furniture tripping me up, its spaniels and furniture polish. I'd just wanted to make it smell more friendly, more like my home.

I concentrated on the job; a yellow van meant someone weak, who tried to attack the family by putting his hand in a box. I gave the full anti-wolf bark and he ran away fast in his van, as always. Easy. Then there was the car that stopped down the road. I gave it full volume. By the end of the day, I was feeling quite pleased with myself when I saw Elodie's car coming back up the lane. I went berserk with excitement but she ignored me completely and went into the house. I followed.

I jumped all over the place with excitement but Elodie just walked away, went into another room and closed the door. Some time later she came out and called me to her. I went like a rocket but the frenzy of first seeing her had gone and I didn't feel like jumping so I just nuzzled her, licked her and enjoyed her caresses.

'We need to talk, Elodie,' her father called from the living room where they'd shut themselves in with the spaniels. Elodie took me into the room with her and sent me to lie in my corner.

'He's gone bonkers without you,' David continued. Elodie sighed. 'He's peed in the kitchen so we had to send him outside and he's done nothing but bark his head off all day. We just can't have that, you know.'

'It's only been a fortnight, Dad. You've got to give him time to adjust. And this is my first day back at work. He'll get used to it and he'll be able to see I'm coming back.' She came over and sat on the floor beside me. 'It's not surprising he's anxious after all he's been through.'

'That's what I mean, love,' her father's voice was kind and reasonable. 'I did warn you that it might be too difficult for you. No-one will think the worse of you if you admit that and I'm sure Izzie will find another home... he's a beautiful, sweet dog - but he's got problems. And we've got to think of other people too. Apart from the neighbours, it's not fair on your mother.'

I waited for Elodie to explain what a good guardian I was. 'I know,' she said. Everything has echoes. You look back and you see the turning points but what makes the hairs rise on your neck is when you see one at the time you are in it. The clock ticked in the silence and a sleeping spaniel farted.

'Elodie's right,' said Adelphe, 'It is only a fortnight. And I don't want to give up on Izzie. What's a little urine and some barking compared with the love of a dog. Look at him.' They looked. 'You can't help loving him. And when I think of what he's been through, it makes my blood boil, it really does. I don't know as much about dogs as you two do but it's a bit like getting married isn't. You have to get used to each other's funny little ways and... adjust a bit. So we've got some adjusting to do and so has Sirius.'

'What do you mean, funny little ways?' demanded David.

'Anyway,' Adelphe rushed on, 'the other thing I wanted to say is that you were going to see this trainer-woman who will help you develop more technique and I think that's a good idea, so you go ahead, dear.'

'It's not that I'd forgotten,' Elodie said slowly, 'it's that it's not so easy to find the right person.'

'Well that's up to you really, isn't it?"

'I think your mother's being very generous Elodie, very

generous. Perhaps your perfect trainer doesn't exist but even if you learn a bit more from someone and ignore the things that aren't right...'

Elodie shook her head firmly. 'It doesn't work like that, Dad. With dog training, just one bit wrong and everything's wrong. And I won't have someone destroy what I've built so far with Izzie. OK, I'll go and look again. And thank you Mum. I needed someone to tell me to keep going. I have been starting to wonder if I've done the right thing. But I do love him so.'

'Which is always a good way to start. In fact, the only way to start,' declared her mother.

I padded after Elodie, determined not to let her out of my sight, and after the pleasures of walking and grooming, I settled beside her as she bashed a computer keyboard. I dozed as she muttered, 'another Behaviourist who thinks we should behave like dogs and bite them back ... a 'dog whisperer' ... like to see someone whisper in the ear of some of the dogs I saw in the S.P.A... 'totally natural training'... so a collar and lead are totally natural are they but a muzzle apparently isn't...'speak to your dog in a language he understands'... oh, not the old 'eating before he does', I'll scream if I hear one more person turning food into rivalry with humans...what will they turn into a 'privilege' next? The air the dog breathes? Do they really think a dog's so stupid he doesn't know that a human is not a dog?!! OK perhaps we can learn some things from the way dogs treat each other but I thought the point was in the inter-species contact not trying to turn me into a dog... barking mad they are.

You won't believe this one! This couple have a problem with a dog territory-marking round the house and this Behaviourist advises them to urinate into bottles, keep the urine in separate bottles for a fortnight then sprinkle drops from the two different bottles round the house. So for a

fortnight the dog carries on as usual, and then, if you accept
the idea that a dog can't tell human pee from dog pee, then
he does what dogs do when they sniff another dog's urine -
he cocks his leg even more! I mean, can you see me asking
Mum and Dad to piddle in bottles, keep it for two weeks,
then sprinkle it on Mum's beloved furniture.' And so she
went on and on for so long, I almost missed the change in
tone.

'That's more like it. No hitting, no shouting… gentle dog
training… but he openly says he uses whatever level of
constraint is necessary… works with difficult and
dangerous… and with puppies…no dog is irrecuperable… it
is never too soon for a dog to learn - nor too late…Michel
Hasbrouck and the dogmasters - sounds like Achilles and the
Myrmidons in that film, or a sixties pop group… pity it's a
man - they can rely on physical strength instead of technique,
because they've got it… but I think this is still the one, and
he trains people to be trainers… Izzie,' I perked up my ears,
'we're going to go and see Michel Hasbrouck. One and a half
days together having fun near Paris. And then I'm going to
keep going until I'm a dogmaster.' Fun sounded good. Dog
training was usually a doddle so that was all right too. My ears
relaxed again. And then grew very very relaxed as slim fingers
massaged the base, getting rid of the little itches in all those
channels between the bones, smoothing the crimped hair on
the ears themselves, teasing a little knot that had appeared
since grooming, just behind my left ear.

'I want to be someone you can look up to,' Elodie told me,
holding my brown stare with her serious hazel eyes. And
there it was. The something Stratoo had worked out but
applied to the wrong Human. The something all dogs want.
Love is the starting point, the only starting point, but we need
to look up to someone. And Elodie would be that someone,
I knew it, with or without this Michel Hasbrouck, whoever

he was. She was more than halfway there, we were more than halfway there together. I thought back over my life, over how I had got here, over 'here'.

If I am lucky, I am only halfway through the great adventure of life. I am still learning about you humans, with your strange ways. And so my story ends, at a new beginning. Of course I can't tell you all this in words so I will do what dogs have always done. I will lay my head on your lap and let you read my eyes. And when my final Choosing comes, just stroke my head as I leave this world and say the words of farewell for me. When you look at the stars, remember me, Sirius of the Soum de Gaia, not such a bad dog after all.

About the Author

I'm a Welsh writer and photographer living in the south of France with a big white dog, a scruffy black dog, a Nikon D750 and a man. I taught English in Wales for many years and my claim to fame is that I was the first woman to be a secondary headteacher in Carmarthenshire. I'm mother or stepmother to five children so life has been pretty hectic.

I've published all kinds of books, both with conventional publishers and self-published. You'll find everything under my name from prize-winning poetry and novels, military history, translated books on dog training, to a cookery book on goat cheese. My work with top dog-trainer Michel Hasbrouck has taken me deep into the world of dogs with problems, and inspired one of my novels. With Scottish parents, an English birthplace and French residence, I can usually support the winning team on most sporting occasions.

MORE BOOKS BY JEAN GILL

The Troubadours Quartet

Winner of The Global Ebook Award for Best Historical Fiction
Book 1 'Song at Dawn'

...by far the best historical fiction novel I have read this year and I don't think another novel can beat this.
Rabia Tanveer, readers' favorite.com

THE TROUBADOURS QUARTET

1150: Provence

On the run from abuse, Estela wakes in a ditch with only her lute, her amazing voice, and a dagger hidden in her underskirt. Her talent finds a patron in Aliénor of Aquitaine and more than a music tutor in the Queen's finest troubadour and Commander of the Guard, Dragonetz los Pros.

Weary of war, Dragonetz uses Jewish money and Moorish expertise to build that most modern of inventions, a papermill, arousing the wrath of the Church. Their enemies gather, ready to light the political and religious powder-keg of medieval Narbonne.

Set in the period following the Second Crusade, Jean Gill's spellbinding romantic thrillers evoke medieval France with breathtaking accuracy. The characters leap off the page and include amazing women like Eleanor of Aquitaine and Ermengarda of Narbonne, who shaped history in battles and in bedchambers.

Chapter 1

She woke with a throbbing headache, cramp in her legs and a curious sensation of warmth along her back. The warmth moved against her as she stretched her stiff limbs along the constraints of the ditch. She took her time before opening her eyes, heavy with too little sleep. The sun was already two hours high in the sky and she was waking to painful proof that her choice of sleeping quarters had been forced.

'I am still alive. I am here. I am no-one,' she whispered. She remembered that she had a plan but the girl who made that plan was dead. Had to be dead and stay dead. So who was she now? She needed a name.

A groan beside her attracted her attention. The strange warmth along her back, with accompanying thick white fur and the smell of damp wool, was easily identified. The girl pushed against a solid mass of giant dog, which shifted enough to let her get herself out of the ditch, where they had curved together into the sides. She recognized him well enough even though she had no idea when he had joined her in the dirt. A regular scrounger at table with the other curs, all named 'Out of my way' or worse. You couldn't mistake this one though, one of the mountain dogs bred to guard the sheep, his own coat shaggy white with brindled parts on his back and ears. Only he wouldn't stay with the flock, whatever anyone tried with him. He'd visit the fields happily enough but at the first opportunity he'd be back at the chateau. Perhaps he thought she was heading out to check on the sheep and that he'd tag along to see what he was missing.

'Useless dog,' she gave a feeble kick in his general direction. 'Can't even do one simple job. They say you're too fond of people to stay in the field with the sheep. Well, I've got news for you about people, you big stupid bastard of a useless dog. Nobody wants you.' She felt tears pricking and smeared them across her cheeks with an impatient, muddy hand. 'And if you've broken this, you'll really feel my boot.' She knelt on the edge of the ditch to retrieve an object completely hidden in a swathe of brocade.

She had counted on having the night to get away but by now there would be a search on. If Gilles had done a good job, they would find her bloody remnants well before there was any risk of them finding her living, angry self. If he had hidden the clues too well, they might keep searching until they really did find her. And if the false trail was found but too obvious, then there would be no let-up, ever. And she would never see Gilles again. She shivered, although the day was already promising the spring warmth typical of the south. She would never see Gilles again anyway, she told herself. He knew the risks as well as she did. And if it had to be done, then she was her mother's daughter and would never - 'Never!' she said aloud - forget that, whoever tried to make her. She was no longer a child but sixteen summers.

All around her, the sun was casting long shadows on the bare vineyards, buds showing on the pruned vine-stumps but no leaves yet. Like rows of wizened cats tortured on wires, the gnarled stumps bided their time. How morbid she had become these last months! Too long a winter and spent in company who considered torture-methods an amusing topic of conversation. Better to look forward. In a matter of weeks, the vines would start to green, and in another two months, the spectacular summer growth would shoot upwards and outwards but for now, all was still wintry grey.

There was no shelter in the April vineyards and the road stretched forward to Narbonne and back towards Carcassonne, pitted with the holes gouged by the severe winter of 1149. Along this road east-west, and the Via Domitia north-south, flowed the life-blood of the region, the trade and treaties, the marriage-parties and the armies, the hired escorts sent by the Viscomtesse de Narbonne and the murderers they were protection against. The girl knew all this and could list fifty fates worse than death, which were not only possible but a likely outcome of a night in a ditch. What she had forgotten was that as soon as she stood up in this open landscape, in daylight, she could see for miles - and be seen.

She looked back towards Carcassonne and chewed her lip. It was already too late. The most important reason why she should not have slept in a ditch beside the road came back to her along with the growing clatter of a large party of horse and, from the sound of it, wagons. The waking and walking was likely to be even more dangerous than the sleeping and it was upon her already.

The girl stood up straight, brushed down her muddy skirts and clutched her brocade parcel to her breast. She knew that following her instinct to run would serve for nothing against the wild mercenaries or, at best, suspicious merchants, who were surely heading towards her. She was lucky to have passed a tranquil night - or so the night now seemed compared with the bleak prospect in front of her. What a fool to rush from one danger straight into another, forgetting the basic rules of survival on the open road. To run now would make her prey so she searched desperately for another option. In her common habit, bedraggled and dirty, she was as invisible as she could hope to be. No thief would look twice at her, nor think she had a purse to cut, far less a ransom waiting at home. No reason to bother her.

What she could not disguise was that, common or not, she was young, female and alone, and the consequences of that had been beaten into her when she was five years old and followed a cat into the forest. Not, of course, that anything bad happened in the forest, where she had lost sight of the cat but instead seen a rabbit's white scut vanishing behind a tree, as she tried to tell her father when he found her. His hard hand cut off her words, to teach her obedience for her own good, punctuated with a graphic description of the horrors she had escaped.

All that had not happened in the dappled light and crackling twigs beneath the canopy of leaves and green needles, visited her nightmares instead, with gashed faces and shuddering laughter as she ran and hid, always discovered. Until now, she *had* obeyed, and it had not been for her own good. Fool that she had been. But no more. Now she would run and hide, and not be discovered.

She drew herself up straight and tall. No, bad idea. Instead, she slumped, as ordinary as she could make herself, and felt through the slit in her dress, just below her right hip, for her other option should a quick tongue fail her. The handle fitted snugly into her hand and her fingers closed round it, reassured. The dagger was safe in its sheath, neatly attached to her under-shift with the calico ties she had laboriously sewn into the fabric in secret candle-light. She had full confidence in its blade, knowing well the meticulous care her brother gave his weapons. As to her capacity to use it, let the occasion be judge. And after that, God would be, one way or another.

By now, the oncoming chink of harness and thud of hooves was so loud that she could hardly hear the low growl beside her. The dog was on his feet, facing the danger. He threw back his head and gave the deep bark of his kind against the wolf. The girl crossed herself and the first horse came into sight.

Lightning Source UK Ltd.
Milton Keynes UK
UKOW04f1700280216

269232UK00001B/15/P